CELEBRATING SECOMBE

The famous
Eccles !!

CELEBRATING SECOMBE

A Tribute to
SIR HARRY SECOMBE

CHRIS GIDNEY

HarperCollins*Publishers*

HarperCollins*Publishers*
77–85 Fulham Palace Road, London W6 8JB
www.**fire**and**water**.com

First published in Great Britain in 2001
by HarperCollins*Publishers*

1 3 5 7 9 10 8 6 4 2

A catalogue record for this book
is available from the British Library.

ISBN 0 00 710778 1

Printed and bound in Great Britain by
Creative Print and Design (Wales), Ebbw Vale

This book is dedicated to Harry and Myra Secombe
from friends, family and fans alike.

Rarely has one person
given so much fun and laughter
to so many.

Contents

Acknowledgements

This has probably been my most difficult yet most satisfying book to write. Not because of its subject – Harry is the best in the world – but because of its unusual format. At times, particularly nearing that terrifying deadline, it felt like the biggest jigsaw in the world laid out in front of me. Would I be able to join all the variously sized pieces together and provide a coherent work that Harry could take pride in? I hoped so.

As Sir Harry himself will tell you, writing a book is like doing a show: you can't do it alone. Therefore I would like to say thank you to every one of those who took the time and effort to contact me with their memories of Harry. Each personal contribution has helped to make this tribute special.

In particular I am grateful to Danny La Rue, Norman Vaughan, Michael Aspel, Wyn Calvin, Vince Hill, the British Actors' Equity Association, Gary Wilmot, Fiona Castle, Guy Bennett, Val Doonican, Angela Morley, Max Geldray, Lin Bennett, *The Stage* newspaper, Dick Baker, Cyril Fletcher, David Lloyd-Jones, Medwyn Hughes, Thora

Hird, Wendy Craig, Pam Rhodes, Doone Ellerton, Ann Bissett, Ruth Madoc, Jeanette Scott, Ray Norwood, Don Maclean, Malcolm Flanagan, Gill Snow, Fred Secombe and Rick Wakeman, for your time, personal encouragement and support in this work.

My thanks to my wife, Trinity, for her belief in the project, even when I was overwhelmed by it; my children, Luke, Anna and Ben, for letting me disappear into the office for days at a time; my PA, Sally, for performing her wonderful Sherlock Holmes impersonation as she tracked down so many hidden people; Jan Korris for helping me to see more clearly into my own life and so into the lives of others; James, my publisher, for his confidence in me; and most of all, to Harry and Myra themselves. For without them, none of this would have been so pleasurable or possible!

In thumbing through hundreds of books in order to find thoughts about Sir Harry from people that I was unable to contact personally, I found, in almost every instance, that 'Secombe' was next to 'Second World War' in the indexes. Rather appropriate, I thought, since Harry not only experienced the war, but almost explodes with laughter everywhere he goes, and blows everyone else apart as he does! I am grateful, therefore, to the following authors and publishers for using their work in the research or for their kind permission to reproduce excerpts included in this book:

Dominic Behan, The Life and Times of Spike Milligan
    (Methuen, 1988) for extracts on pp. 108, 112, 122 and 134
Michael Bentine, The Reluctant Jester *(Bantam Press, 1992)*
    © *Michael Bentine, 1992. Published by Bantam Press, a*

*division of Transworld Publishers. All rights reserved. For
extracts on pp. 181 and 196*

Ronald Bergan, The Great Theatres of London *(Prion
Books, 1990)*

Roy Castle, Now and Then *(Robson Books, 1994) for
extracts on pp. 96, 99, 130 and 232*

Peter Cotes, Sincerely Dickie *(Robert Hale Ltd, 1989) for
extract on p. 70*

Val Doonican, Walking Tall *(Elm Tree Books, 1986) for
extract on p. 140*

Lord Delfont, Curtain Up! *(Robson Books, 1989)*

Norma Farnes, The Goons: The Story *(Virgin Books, 1997)*

Cyril Fletcher, Nice One Cyril! *(Oasis, 1989)*

Cleo Laine, Cleo *(Simon & Schuster/Faith Evans Associates,
1994) for extract on p. 241*

Gary Morecambe and Martin Stirling, Morecambe and
Wise: Behind the Sunshine, *(Robson Books, 1994) for
extract on p. 56*

Frank Muir, A Kentish Lad *(Bantam Press, 1997)* © *Frank
Muir, 1997. Published by Bantam Press, a division of
Transworld Publishers. All rights reserved. For extract on
p. 208.*

Lord Rix, Farce About Face *(Hodder & Stoughton, 1989) for
extract on p. 168*

David Roper, Bart *(Pavilion Books, 1994) for extract on
pp. 122–3*

Harry Secombe, Zoo Loo Book *(Robson Books, 1999) for
extracts on pp. 18 and 64*

Graham Stark, Remembering Peter Sellers *(Robson Books,
1991)*

Joan Sutherland, A Prima Donna's Progress *(Weidenfeld
and Nicolson, 1997) for extract on p. 56*

Norman Wisdom, 'Cos I'm a Fool *(Breedon Books, 1996) for
extract on p. 51*

In gathering all the many and various pieces of information and stories about Harry, I may have inadvertently forgotten to credit somebody, and would be happy to set the record straight in future editions of this volume.

Introduction

Each time I have met Sir Harry Secombe he has impressed me. Not because of his quick wit. Not because of his huge personality. Not because of his generosity. He has impressed me simply because despite the laughter, he is real.

Many celebrities are driven by insecurity to hide behind masks of varying kinds; not so Harry. What you see is what you get, as the tributes in this celebration will show. He is one of the most genuine, sincere and humble men I have ever met. Yet he knows how to use his gifts in such an effective way that he has been at the top of the show business ladder for more than fifty years.

My first encounter came when I escorted Mary Millar up to Great Ormond Street Hospital for Children. She was to be a guest on one of Harry's Sunday programmes. Mary, having spent a lifetime in the business, had just left *Phantom of the Opera* to create her role of Rose in the BBC comedy *Keeping Up Appearances*. Working alongside the redoubtable Mrs Bouquet had been quite an experience for Mary, and she was unusually nervous that cold autumn morning as we drove into town.

Mary loved children and was anxious at the suffering she expected to see at this great hospital, yet concerned to give of her best in support of Harry's show. What's more, the programme was due to be transmitted live. Hearts beat more rapidly at the prospect of a live broadcast. When a programme is recorded, it's easy to stop and begin again if you find yourself tongue-tied or lost for words. So many programmes are recorded these days that hearing the word 'live' sends a shock of electricity through a performer's brain. And it was also the first time that she was to talk publicly about her private life and her strong faith.

Arriving among the tangled cables of the outside-broadcast vans, we were ushered across a sea of wires and cameras to the café area where her piece with Harry was to be transmitted. Initially unsure of where to put ourselves, but smiling apprehensively around the room, we suddenly heard the familiar cry of 'Hello there!' echo across the hospital ward.

In had burst Harry, with a beam across his face that banished tensions and fears in the split second of his arrival. After a hug from what seemed to be a long-lost brother, the ice within Mary had melted; she instantly relaxed and was giggling away with her host. Harry explained the format, and they were soon so eloquently engaged in the job that I felt like an unwanted appendage. Watching on a nearby monitor, I was impressed with the way in which Harry made all his guests not only relax off camera, but on screen too.

It was several years later, as I sat by Mary's bed in London's Bart's Hospital, that we recalled the story. Mary was now suffering from severe cancer suddenly and traumatically contracted while working on Disney's London show, *Beauty and the Beast*. She knew her future, and that she would not recover from her illness, but remembered

Harry's kindness that day and started laughing about how his sense of humour had produced such a calming influence on her. It was in the saddest moments of her illness that laughter helped sustain her.

After nearly six hours awaiting the all-clear to make the final trip back home, her husband Rafael appeared to say that the doctors had apologized for the extended wait. Apparently the reason for this was that their 'discharge' meeting had overrun. Surrounded by the bottles, bedpans, drips and buckets of the ward, it was certainly the funniest word he could have used.

'Harry would have liked that one!' Mary giggled. It's true. It could have come straight out of a *Goon Show* sketch, but demonstrates the lasting impression made by the man nicknamed 'Neddy'.

My most recent meeting with Harry was as remarkable as the first. I had barely got out of the car when I saw a jovial figure standing by his front door, giggling uncontrollably. The smiling welcome at the door, the greeting like a long-lost friend, the quips and laughter that emanated as I followed Lord and Lady Secombe down the corridor were like an invigorating tonic.

The beautiful house in which they live is huge, yet has an air of cosiness and tranquillity. The view from the front room across many miles of the Surrey Downs is stunning, and is a constant reminder of the distance Harry's life and career has spanned.

Although the house seems too big for just the two of them, it suits their personalities perfectly. Large but not imposing. Spacious but not indifferent. Grand but definitely not aloof. Harry and Myra have their feet planted firmly on the ground.

In researching this book, everyone I have had the pleasure of meeting and talking to has mentioned both of them.

It's never just 'Harry', always 'Harry and Myra'. They are a pair. A strength and support to each other, and the best example of a happy marriage that I have ever come across. On the day of their marriage, when they promised to love in 'sickness and in health', they meant it.

Despite Harry's stroke leaving one side incapacitated, he is the same happy joker, yet reluctantly he understands his new limitations. However, 'limitations' is not one of Harry's favourite words, and not one that he has associated with his career, which has extended over many years and several generations. The stage, theatre, radio, television and films have all enjoyed Harry's stamp of originality. The Goons were a major part of his life, but without overshadowing everything else. In fact many would comment that his solo career has been bigger than the famed radio series, which just goes to show what a talented man he is.

Although offering a potted version of Harry's life journey, this volume is not intended as a detailed, historic account, but is a celebration of the man, by the people who really know him. A collage of memories, poems, prayers and laughter commemorates the two sides of Harry: his personal life and his public life. Both are closely entwined, as the following tributes disclose. He is loved as much by those who have never met him as he is by his close friends and family. Also recorded here are comments on Harry from some of those we have sadly lost, but who were obviously impressed by him.

His life has not been the charmed existence that many may presume, and his struggles have at times been overwhelming, particularly his battle in recent years against illnesses that have severely restricted him. The fears, depression and self-doubt have strengthened his feeling for life, however, and given him the ability to draw alongside others with empathy. Harry has always been less concerned with things than with people and yet has remained true to his stature in the profession.

Harry once joked that the meaning of a star these days has changed.

'A star today is anyone strong enough to hold a microphone. Then you have the superstar, who is the one who has shaken hands with the great impresario, Sir Bernard Delfont.

'Then you have the super-duper star. He's the one who has refused to shake hands with Sir Bernard Delfont!'

This volume unwraps why one of the country's greatest comedians is so loved and respected, and why it is true to say that Harry is a real star who has shone brightly into the lives of so many, and made a huge difference.

It's all credit to Harry that even those who have not met him describe him as 'a really nice man'; such is the effect of his personality. This is quite an astonishing statement: people would not usually be so certain about somebody they haven't even shaken hands with. It's wonderful, however, in an age when some comedy seems committed to debasing and humiliating the human race, to have something as 'old-fashioned' as Harry's simple decency, which obviously bridges the footlights and transcends the screen.

During the preparation of this volume, it's been lovely to see how many of those I have interviewed either sent their personal regards to Sir Harry, or promised to make contact themselves. I know it's been a real source of frustration for Harry that his illness prevents him from giving in the same way that he is used to. However, giving and receiving is a two-way operation, and maybe it is time for Harry to be on the receiving end for a change. Perhaps this book can make a start.

Chris Gidney
October 2000

Schoolboy Secombe

I think you can laugh at almost anything so long as it doesn't hurt anybody.

HARRY SECOMBE

If you asked Harry to recall the most terrifying moment in all his fifty years in show business there would be all manner of things that he could mention. He may decide it was the fear of forgetting those first few emotionally quickened lines of 'If I Ruled the World' in front of millions of television viewers. Surely it would be the nerve-wrenching audition at the infamous Windmill Theatre in London, or the opening night of *Pickwick* on Broadway? Perhaps most of all, it would be the horrifying thought of nobody laughing. For this is what Sir Harry has undoubtedly 'built his house' on.

Human beings are the only living creatures with the ability to laugh. Tigers, elephants, ants, gnus and even laughing hyenas can't actually titter, gurgle and hoot like we can. It's fortunate, therefore, that Harry Secombe was not destined to be a vet.

1

Just like the old television advert for Opal Fruits that happily declared 'Made to make your mouth water!', Harry was made to make us laugh. And he has done so for more than fifty years. Not only does he make us laugh, he laughs himself, and when it happens, it's like a mini-explosion of delight. That sudden overflow of hilarity, a gushing amalgamation of giggle and chuckle, suddenly pours out of him like a waterfall, bringing refreshment, as a living tonic. And it happens on a regular basis; one could count the number of laughs a minute as one does a typist's word speed. You might expect Harry to be on a mountaintop singing a serious aria, or waiting for a bus, or shopping in Sainsbury's, only to burst into an instantaneous fit of laughter.

A world without laughter for Harry would be hell; he would simply not survive it. Giggles, titters, chuckles, shrieks, hysterics and chortles have not only kept his troubles in proportion, but made his life worth living. This amusement is not a ploy to avoid the reality of pain – tears and laughter have often been intermingled – but a practical tool enabling him and others to overcome many of life's major hurdles.

Harry's chuckling laugh makes him a wonderful person to be around. There is nobody in the close world of showbiz who has a bad word to say about him. On the contrary, most have considered it a privilege to be around him because of the genuine joy his presence brings into the lives of those he has contact with. Yet, unlike the lives of other 'saintly' figures which we suppose must have been rather boring, Harry's has been the opposite of dull. He has lived one of the most exciting, engaging and successful lives one could imagine, but one that has always been filled with laughter.

In a profession renowned for its high divorce rate, Harry says that laughter is the secret of his happy marriage to

Myra that has lasted more than forty years. Laughter, he says, is the reason he has stayed at the top of the business for several decades, and the explanation for his ability to transfer himself from stage to screen and back again.

He's not one to poke fun at another's misfortune; as often as not, the laughs are at his own expense. His weight, his looks, his acting, and his golf have all been targets for the Secombe send-up. Yet when he does this, although everyone around laughs heartily, no one takes him seriously. They have too high a regard for the man who has brought so much pleasure to so many for so long.

Who hasn't experienced the deep healing a laugh can bring? Is there anyone on earth who has not been able to face the pressure of tomorrow after the recharging laughter of today? For Sir Harry, the key to life is laughter.

The first memory that Harry's brother Fred has of him is of someone who was 'endlessly laughing'. Fred Secombe was born nearly three years before his brother, and yet his first and most abiding memory of Harry more than seventy-five years later is the way in which Harry made him chuckle so easily. 'Harry, myself and our mother were out shopping and Harry was already starting to imitate those around him. When this poor man with a crooked back came towards us, Harry, only four years old but already renowned for his clever ability to mimic, immediately went into his Hunchback of Notre Dame impression. Seeing him dragging his feet and foaming at the mouth, my mother was mortified, and immediately clipped him around the ear for his efforts. She gave me a stern look too as I tried to stifle my own guffaws. Harry was never directly rude or intentionally badly behaved, but our mother swore she would never take him shopping again after that!'

Fred was the eldest and was followed several years later by a sister, who died when she was four of complicated appendicitis. It was a terrible shock to the family but a wonderful example of the care shown by his parents, who absorbed much of the emotional impact themselves and in so doing spared their remaining children the enormous trauma of the event. Despite the fact that he was very devoted to her, Fred admits that even today, he cannot remember anything about Joan, so effectively did his parents shield him from the pain.

It was in this loving home that Harry made his first public appearance on 8 September 1921, giving an admirable debut performance with a vast squeal from the pair of lungs that were later to become famous for their ability to belt out the highest, longest and loudest notes. Indeed 1921 was the year of many a first appearance, including that of the first full-length Charlie Chaplin film, *The Kid*. Women everywhere were starting to swoon over screen heart-throb Rudolph Valentino, and Marie Stopes opened her first birth-control clinic in the UK.

Babies continued to arrive at the Secombe home, however, and Carol came along when Harry was barely one. She, like her predecessors, quickly embraced the musical atmosphere and very soon all three children shared a deep appreciation of comedy and song. This was the natural consequence of being part of a family with a musical heritage, headed by a grandfather who had been singing in Hereford Cathedral for many years. Grandfather Secombe had once hit a personal crisis when, for some unexplained reason, he suddenly lost his voice altogether in the middle of a concert. Even stranger, one year later it had suddenly returned, several octaves lower. Wondering if in fact his voice had broken twice, he was nonetheless extremely proud of his new bass baritone.

Harry had showbiz in his blood; Uncle George played in the Keskersays Dance Band at the Langland Bay Hotel, and

Aunt Mary played the piano in Woolworth's to amuse the shoppers.

Harry, Fred and Carol were also surrounded by the jokes and sketches favoured by their father, Frederick Ernest, who always put them to good use in a local amateur capacity. It was in the home, however, that he would first try out his interpretation of various monologues, often over the family dinner table:

So you want a railway story
While you wait for the London train?
It's a story I've never told, sir,
So I'll tell it to you again

We were going a mile a minute
And we stepped out on to the line
The driver said we're due, sir
At eleven sixty-nine.

All of a sudden then came
The sound of a mighty crash
You could hear the shrieks of survivors
And I thought of the ready cash.

I saw a sweet young lady
In a mashed potato state
Her final words to me were
Porter, is my hat on straight?

He would then regale the giggling family with music-hall songs that Harry would emulate while lying in bed, long after dark. His room-mate Fred would be kept awake by such renditions until a parental voice called out for 'less noise and more sleep now, boys!'

Much excitement was generated when a second-hand piano arrived in their home one day. Somehow their parents had managed to save for this block of wobbly timber and ivory which was to provide the family with great pleasure on many a winter's evening. Later, it was superseded by a Rediffusion set, a rented wireless that brought even more Secombe favourites into the home.

> Little Willy had a football, that would make all his
>   playmates stare
> But Willy filled it up with gas, instead of with some
>   air
> A bobby took it from him, just for playing in the street
> And later on that evening, he went to take a seat
> He sat down on that football, and it went off like a
>   gun
> They found his feet, way up the street
> And his day's work was done.

When he wasn't rehearsing his favourite monologues, their father would earn the family's keep as a travelling salesman. Commuting many miles in a day, he would arrive home in the early evening having sold his huge baskets of groceries in the secluded valleys of western Wales. Despite a lack of money, he was a happy, contented man and created a cheerful and close family. Having been to art school when he was younger, he was at one time commissioned to draw the cartoons for the *South Wales Evening Post*.

Their mother is described as a wonderful, caring woman with an expansive sense of humour. She was always there for her three children and supplemented the family's small income with bookkeeping assignments for a few local firms. She had been blessed with a delightfully full soprano voice, but an operation on her nose had destroyed her voice's inner resonance and she was unable to sing after that. Yet she never failed to encourage her children to use their voices.

When they were young, Harry and sister Carol's similar sense of humour brought them increasingly close. Spending hours rehearsing versions of their father's tunes and monologues, they soon developed a comic double act which they would perform at any given opportunity. Harry always seemed to be very shy, a common link between many comedians. Harry himself started off by being what he calls the 'regimental berk' at home, progressing to being the 'school twit'. It was a self-defence mechanism, getting the bullies to laugh rather than having to fight them.

Yet the opportunity to perform a favourite song soon enabled him to overcome his uncertainties. Family, friends and eventually the local social clubs watched the double act with great delight, but arguments over their material caused Fred much frustration. On the way to the cinema one day Harry and Carol were squabbling so much that neither heard their brother's pleas to stop. Fred decided the only way to make them listen was to walk back home without them, and so miss the film. It took a few moments for Harry and Carol to realize that Fred was now walking in the opposite direction, and they were so surprised at what he was doing that they stopped fighting. At least for a while.

School was soon on the agenda and with Fred leading the way, Harry was enrolled in St Thomas's School, just a short distance away. Before long Harry was energetically involved in school life; his favourite possession was his jockey cap, a peaked hat he was so fond of that he would often sleep in it.

St Leger's Crescent was the Secombes' second home; they had moved there when Harry was four years old. Their house was at the top of a very steep hill, with another hill covered with woods stretching on and upwards behind it.

The view that Harry had when he emerged from his front door each day was superb. Being at the top of the hill, he was afforded a panoramic view of three landscapes that in a way prefigured his life to come. Turning to his right he would immediately recognize the steep valleys whose green sides no doubt reminded him of his Welsh roots. The huge spire of the local parish church speared heavenwards and was perhaps symbolic of his own faith as he looked straight forward. The docks, opened by the Prince and Princess of Wales in 1881, spread out to his left and a huge expanse of sea met the sky as he lifted his eyes upwards. It was possible on a clear day to see across the coast to Somerset and Cornwall, whose tourist resorts would one day beckon for him to star in their summer shows.

No thought of this now, as little Harry ran across the road to the 'patch', the local name for a piece of scrubland upon which the children from the estate could safely play all manner of games, cricket being the favourite. Teams were formed against each other in a spirit of enthusiastic seriousness. 'Cloggy' Hayman was the only local child with a full-sized bat, shortened by some thoughtful adult so that the little boy could use it more easily.

Marbles, like conkers and football, had its season. Prized glass baubles were examined, discussed and swapped with all the solemnity of a proper business venture, but it wasn't always the biggest ones that won the all-important matches. The tiny glass strikers were deadly in the right hands, and could knock over a whole pile of marbles.

While the tiny army of local offspring played, mothers would chat over gateposts, comparing notes on how well their respective children were doing at school. Mrs Jones was one of those mothers, feared by many a small boy for her fiery temper and constant chatting. Once she started, you really couldn't get away until she had told you all the local gossip. When she called on the Secombe home one afternoon, it was Harry's idea to dive under the kitchen table to avoid her. With a cup of tea on the table, Mrs Jones began to discuss the issues of the day with their mother, while two little boys lay trembling beneath her, hoping she wouldn't drop anything that would cause her to glance beneath the cloth, and wondering how long she was going to stay. Holding their breath for fear of being discovered, they suspected Mother already knew. Their suspicions were proved correct when over an hour later, at the sound of the closing front door, Harry and Fred emerged with stiff limbs only to be severely reprimanded by their mother for being so rude. As they stood there with little white faces, they could detect a tiny crease beside their mother's mouth as she spoke which seemed to hide a desire to chuckle.

Harry was a dedicated prankster, always looking for the next available laugh, but he always managed to stop short of being really naughty. No matter what tricks he got up to, corporal punishment was never on the agenda. Never a hand was lifted against the brood and yet they held both their parents in deep respect. A look, a word and the threat of being sent to bed early were all that was needed to keep them in order.

One day when Harry came home after being caned by his teacher for stupidity, his father roused himself and headed straight for the school in readiness for battle. Harry had suffered a serious bout of scarlet fever that had badly affected his eyesight, and was unable to see the blackboard. Determined to make a strong protest over this unauthorized attack on his son, Frederick marched towards the red-brick school in disgust. Upon his arrival, Mr Minty was nowhere to be seen – the rather irritable teacher was apparently in hiding – but Harry's father's annoyance was clearly imparted to the head, and it never happened again. Mr Minty seemed to have a forte for beating boys, for another parent was also seen storming across the 'patch' one day, sleeves rolled up in readiness. 'I'll get that Mr Minty,' she screamed as onlookers stood watching with open mouths, 'I'll tear him limb from limb and put his lights out, I will!'

Dynevor was a converted municipal secondary school hidden behind the shops of Swansea High Street. The tall, imposing brick building beckoned those who managed to pass their eleven-plus. Those who didn't stayed on at St Thomas's Junior until they reached fourteen, when they would leave as quickly as possible and search for work in one of the local factories or coal mines. Despite the boys' reputation for high jinks and pranks, both passed their scholarship papers with ease, and Harry followed Fred into Dynevor Secondary School a year later. Harry was particularly surprised at his good fortune, and always relished the daily half-hour walk to school with his elder brother.

Fred's patience was often stretched to the limit by his smaller brother's determination to turn every moment into an opportunity for laughter. 'I was sometimes embarrassed when we bumped into friends on the way home because I never knew what Harry was going to say or do!' Their journey home would take them over the city's main bridge spanning the River Fawe, and on their way up to St Leger's Crescent they would pass the fish and chip shop, where for the twopence their mum had given them they could purchase a whole bag of steaming goodies.

Mildred was the name of Harry's first real girlfriend. She lived just across the 'patch', and it was a purely platonic liaison. 'My first girlfriend had a "chuckle line" just below her thigh. I called it that because if I got my hand past there

I was laughing!' So goes the old comic's reflective line on relationships in the early thirties.

Despite his fondness for Mildred, Harry was much more concerned about Ronnie Jones, his best pal who lived six doors away up the road. Ronnie had a defect in the roof of his mouth and the strange noises he made fascinated Harry. Ronnie's speech was so distorted that it was often difficult to understand what he was saying, but while other boys teased him, Harry befriended this unfortunate schoolmate.

After a while Fred became head prefect at Dynevor, which meant he would be needed in school earlier than the other boys. Seizing the opportunity to stay behind in bed that little bit longer, Harry would often rely on his brother's mercy when he arrived at school well after the bell. 'He would plead with me to wipe his name off the official late list to avoid punishment,' remembers Fred. 'I had no trouble at getting up, even at the crack of dawn. Unfortunately Harry was the opposite. He hated getting up in the morning. He still does!'

Weekends were a valued opportunity for Harry to delay his daily appearance, except when fun was on offer. The family indulged in all sorts of sporting activities, as well as the occasional sortie to Swansea Bay where the quality of the sand and the curve of the beach, stretching all the way from the Mumbles Lighthouse to Porthcawl fifteen miles away, has been compared to the Bay of Naples. Unlike Naples, however, the shore was full of industrial enterprises whose effluent was pumped straight into the sea. It was just as well for Fred that he was not allowed in the water due to a rheumatic rash that caused his legs to seize up. Harry, on the other hand, splashed in and out with glee.

On occasional Saturdays the boys would be invited out on one of the tugboats down by Swansea Docks. 'One of our friends called Tom invited us out on his boat as a treat one day,' recalls Fred. 'It wasn't really a treat for me because I was violently seasick all day. Mam had packed us a lunch that I just wasn't able to touch. Harry obligingly ate my sandwiches with a playful grin.'

Llechryd, notably one of the most difficult places for an Englishman to pronounce, was where the family holidays were taken. They would arrive on the train at this pretty little village nestling on the banks of the river Teifi about five miles from Cardigan. It was here that Grandpa and Grandma Bloom resided. Grandpa Bloom was of Norwegian descent and operated his own mill that ground the corn to supply the beautiful bread, the smell of which seemed to fill the air for miles around when Grandma Bloom was baking. Harry, Fred and Carol couldn't wait to get their teeth into the array of loaves on offer, and spread the home-made butter that instantly melted on the wonderfully warm crusty bread. A few pigs and prize vegetables completed a smallholding that seemed like a huge farm to the smaller members of the Secombe family. Home-cooked ham with home-grown potatoes and laver bread made with seaweed was the speciality, followed by bread pudding. It was heaven on earth for the young Harry, who was always a connoisseur of good food.

Apart from the feasts, the most exciting event of the holiday was when Grandpa Bloom would start the car up. Being used as they were to walking everywhere, the excitement of sitting in the open-topped vehicle rumbling down to the sea at Aberporth was unimaginable. After a week of filling tummies, sea air and exercise, the family would pick nuts to take home to store in readiness for Christmas.

Back home, Sunday School outings were always memorable, particularly on Bank Holiday Monday at Whitsun. All the local churches would combine for a big parade on

Whit Sunday, led by the Salvation Army in full uniform with gleaming brass instruments. The Whitsun treat saw thirty or so excited families climbing on to the steam train for the four-mile journey out into the countryside. The noise of excited children's chatter on the train was almost unbearable, but was calmed twenty minutes later as one by one they disembarked into the greenery.

Proudly garbed in his new Whitsun suit one year, it wasn't long before Harry was hopping over the large cow-pats in the field which, much to the disgust of the adults, each and every schoolboy took great delight in examining. Harry must finally have jumped too high and too far, as with a loud yell, he slipped down the bank and straight into the river. He spent the rest of the outing sitting in the field wrapped in a towel, watching his new clothes drying on a tree. People smiled as they walked past the little figure clutching a mug of tea and still beaming happily behind glasses held together with sticking plaster from last year's accident.

Sundays themselves were always the same, and the repetition was viewed as an anchor to steady the rest of the week. St Thomas's Church was at the bottom of their road, its spire visible for miles around, its bells announcing the start of each service. Communion at eight o'clock was always entertaining, as Mr Allen's large stomach was famous for its loud rumbling. Thinking it was the onset of thunder, visitors could be seen glancing out of the windows and cursing the fact that they had forgotten their umbrellas. It was difficult for the boys to retain their composure for the solemn Communion ritual with Mr Allen's performance echoing around the church.

Other characters who would not have seemed out of place in the BBC's sitcom, *The Vicar of Dibley*, included Mrs Hancock, who possessed a long scraggy turtle neck with a voice to match. The shrieks that came from the woman repeatedly distracted the rest of the congregation, who would constantly struggle to find the right pitch. Most of the children would be watching with much amusement and secretly laying bets as to whether the glasses perched right on the tip of her beaky nose would eventually drop off.

If you were called upon to pump up the organ, it would be seen as a very important, if not emotionally hazardous exercise. For if you allowed the air box to run out of air, it would produce a loud burping noise instead of notes, and would be a talking point for weeks to come.

The day continued with the main morning service at 11 a.m., Sunday School at 3 p.m. and Evensong at 6 p.m. It was a busy day. Apparently the services had originally been designed by the Church of England to fit in with the work of the dairy farmers, who finished milking their cows by eleven. The evening service at 6.30 originated when churches first started to use electric lighting. A service after dark would be a special attraction to experience the new method of lighting. For the young Harry, church was to prove fertile ground for the talents that would be revealed to the world many years later.

It wasn't long before a morning Sunday School was introduced at St Thomas's. At last there was a meeting that was just for the children. It was here that the seeds of Fred's future career were sown, when he was asked to teach the other youngsters. He was also asked to read the lesson, thankfully in English; Swansea was already too cosmopolitan to retain the Welsh language of its outskirts, although basic Welsh was taught at school, enabling Harry and Fred to greet passers-by.

Soon afterwards, having been inspired by a visiting Ugandan speaker, and at the tender age of fourteen, Fred decided to become a priest. By seventeen he had been accepted by the local bishop. If Harry had any thoughts of a vocation based in church life, it was definitely the singing. Closing his eyes in order to focus on the voice of Choirmaster 'Wardy's' wife, Harry's head would spin with the sweetness of the weekly anthem she sang as the church soloist. 'Lead me Lord … lead me in your righteousness' was a particular favourite that the boys would repeatedly sing in their beds until late into the night.

Harry's love of singing was reinforced when he and Fred were accepted into the church choir. Harry relished the ceremonial side of church life, and particularly enjoyed leading the choir out from the vestry complete in surplice, cassock and white clip-on collar. This would serve as his first costume as he walked proudly into the wooden pews facing each other on either side. In the summer the sun would come through the stained-glass window and hit him like a spotlight.

After a good few rousing tunes, sung with all the passion a Welsh boy could muster, the choir would settle down to listen to the preacher. While the songs brought much delight to the young Harry, the down side was always the sermons.

These were long and monotonous, served up by a vicar who had been there for more than thirty-two years, and it's not surprising that the youngsters' thoughts would quickly wander. Apparently the yearly sequence of sermons reached its climax on Advent Sunday, when they started all over again. After attending for a couple of years, Fred and Harry realized that the same reflections were being taught once again, together with the same stories and illustrations.

While Harry sat like a stone to listen to this hopeless preacher, he would start to memorize the sermons by heart, and use them for his own comical ends. Who knows what scripts, situation comedy and characters were being secretly developed during that weekly half-hour of tedium?

Becoming an expert at secretly talking sideways to the boy next to him, Harry also wrote and passed covert notes along the row of choirboys using a sleight of hand comparable to that of the best magicians. The sweets Harry smuggled into church also helped dull some of the agony, but he had to be careful not to rustle the papers too much and risk the choirmaster spotting him. The position of the choir pews afforded a view of the back of the preacher's head, but although the thought undoubtedly travelled through Harry's mind on several occasions, it was too far to flick a discarded wrapper. Below the preacher's back hung an enormous bottom that gave rise to the boys' vulgar and rather unkind nickname of 'Basket Ass'. The yellow nicotine stain on his fingers matched sickly teeth and the stale fragrance of smoke, clear indications that he was a heavy chain smoker.

The end of the First World War had produced an acute need for clerics, and this former carpenter had applied to train for the priesthood via a kind of crash course. The Licentiate in Divinity had been established in order to train vicars as rapidly as possible, but the 'LD', as it was known, was soon given the sarcastic nickname of 'Lamp of the Donkeys'. In the hasty desire to provide churches with ministers, the result of the course was that its graduates often fell short of expectations, their sermons holding absolutely no relevance to everyday life.

In the tedious circumstances it's a wonder that Harry's strong faith ever took root at all. Yet gazing beyond the preacher's platform, he could see one of the magnificent stained-glass windows that adorned the church. Flanked by two gargoyles that may have reminded him of his schoolteachers, the window shone with a heavenly brilliance.

Depicted in radiant reds and blues, three biblical characters illustrated the words Faith, Charity and Hope. Despite the boredom and frustration of the sermons, these three virtues were to become embedded within Harry's own soul, forming the bedrock of his future life.

Above the three characters were a similar number of brightly coloured angels watching those below, but Harry had his own angel. For if he cared to look up above his pew, there was the stone-carved face of a graceful being, smiling down on him as he sang.

Today, that same church has changed very little. St Leger's Crescent still sweeps down to meet St Thomas's Parish Church at its foot. It's such a steep hill that Harry and his brother could almost have rolled down it, and would probably have carried straight on into the churchyard were it not for the ornate metal fence surrounding it.

It still has the feeling of a very close-knit community; as Fred remarked, 'So close, you couldn't change your socks without everyone else knowing.' The stranger is immediately recognized by the children playing in the street, but instantly ignored, assumed to be yet another Secombe fan making a pilgrimage to his idol's place of origin. The current inhabitants at 7 St Leger's Crescent are just as non-plussed when the stranger calls. 'Oh yes, we've had lots of people popping in to say hello,' the woman of the house somewhat wearily replies. 'Thing is, there's not much here for them to see. There's no blue plaque on the wall or anything, but we've spent a lot of money doing the place up so it looks nice. After all, he is a national hero, isn't he?'

Ask any Welshman or Welshwoman on the street and you get the same reply. 'Oh yes, we're very proud of him, you know.'

Harry in turn has always been proud to be Welsh, never attempting to hide his accent or to cover his roots. Though he was somewhat taken aback by the enormous reception he got when bringing *Pickwick* to Cardiff – it was booked weeks ahead – he was delighted with the love shown by his fellow countrymen. It was as if they were personally welcoming him back home.

The willingness to keep a welcome in the hillsides for Harry has extended to his fellow show business compatriots, and Wales has certainly created many of those. International stars claim Harry like a member of their own family.

Sir Anthony Hopkins

Wales's most famous Hollywood star, Sir Anthony has been a fan of Harry's for many a year and remembers their earliest days together.

He is one of the great entertainers and comedians of our time. Like millions of people in Britain I am an avid fan of *The Goon Show* and everything else he has done.

In the summer of 1970, I first met Harry having a lunchtime drink in the Castle pub in North Acton, close to the BBC rehearsal centre. I was at the bar getting my well-earned pint of best bitter, when Harry called out to me with such affection and warmth that I was quite taken by surprise; I had no idea he would know me, but apparently he had seen me in some TV play that had been shown that week.

'We're not doing too badly, boyo, are we? Two boys from Wales!' His voice, and the great joyful belly-laugh that only Harry could produce (a laugh that could stop the Rhondda Express in its tracks), cut through the noisy pub atmosphere on that hot, smoke-filled summer afternoon so long ago. 'Great life, isn't it, bach? Better than working for a living!' This was followed by another great hoot and guffaw of friendliness and Pickwickian bonhomie. That was my first encounter with the Great Secombe.

Harry is a great humanitarian, a blessed and beautiful human being; a powerful example of great but gentle humour and self-mockery in a profession that sometimes takes itself a little too seriously.

Harry is, and ever shall be, a life-affirming tonic for us all.

God bless you, Harry Secombe, for all that you have given us.

Max Boyce

Increasing the perception that all Welsh performers are great singers, Max shares Harry's powerful voice and remembers when his hero made a particular impression in London.

At a variety club tribute dinner to Harry, I was asked to say a few words. In Cardiff's City Hall, the great and the good of the principality of Wales attended in order to honour one of its greatest sons. I spoke about the day I was in concert at the Royal Albert Hall in London.

I turned up for rehearsals and a sound check in the afternoon, when the production manager called me over. 'Mr Boyce, welcome to the Albert Hall. We had one of your fellow countrymen here last week, Harry Secombe. The night before we also had the heavy rock band The Who. They turned up with their entourage

19

overnight. Four articulated lorries, fifteen technicians and roadies with huge graphic equaliser desks, two twenty-four channel mixing desks, miles of cable and banks of loudspeakers.

'Harry Secombe turned up with only his voice, a gift from God. He stood on the stage and sang "Jerusalem" without even a microphone and, do you know, Mr Boyce, there were people standing at the very back of this great auditorium. Right at the back they were, and do you know ... they never heard a bloody thing...'

It goes without saying that Sir Harry is one of the most genuine people I have ever met. It is a privilege to know him and his family and I am proud to call him an old friend. I will always treasure the times Harry and I have spent together, and be forever grateful for his help and encouragement when I was but a rising star in his firmament.

The Grand Theatre, Swansea

Since the demise of Swansea's Empire Theatre, the Grand has taken on the mantle of being the region's major live venue. Touring, ballet, opera and major pantomime productions are all part of its artistic policy. Harry has played here, in his home-town theatre, in all manner of shows, as both theatre manager Gary Iles, and Wendy Weaver, principal of the dance school, remember.
Wendy recalls:

A couple of years ago I was asked by a TV company to allow them to film inside my small terraced house in William Street, situated close to the theatre, which backs on to Swansea's Vetch Field football ground – the home of Swansea City Football Club.

It transpired that Sir Harry's grandparents had lived in my house for many years, and their grandson was a frequent visitor, especially when there was a football game scheduled, because the back garden proffered a free 'grandstand' view over the fence!

We spent a hectic, hilarious morning filming with Sir Harry and listening to his reminiscences and anecdotes. He described the house as it used to be. It brought many memories back to him and every so often he would go off into one of his infectious fits of the giggles which soon had everyone joining in.

He was accompanied by Lady Myra, his wife and a lovely lady. Between us we kept the tea and coffee flowing for everyone. Sir Harry was good-humoured and friendly throughout. Both he and Lady Myra made themselves very much at home and I have a treasured photograph of both of them comfortably ensconced on my sofa, relaxed and happy!

Theatre manager Gary says: I have met Harry five or six times during the ten years I have worked at our theatre and he and Lady Myra have always been charming, friendly, down to earth and full of fun. In short he is a lovely, warm, gentle man.

David Lloyd Jones

As a director and drama teacher in Swansea, David has grown up in Harry's town and knows how fondly the people of Wales think of 'their' Sir Harry. These two pieces were written by his students at Gorseinon College of Performing Arts for Eastside, *a production devised at the college and based on the community where Harry grew up.*

Life on the Eastside

There's the sun hanging in the sky
Looking over the people and their different lives.
Looking down over a town
The place that we call home.

Smoke from the rooftops
Lights in the windows
People in the streets with a downcast attitude.

Life on the East Side, life on the Eastside –
A place where the people know the people who know
  people just like you.
There's a sound hanging in the air
The hustle and the bustle of people everywhere.
Busy lives, striving to survive
In the place that we still call home.

Smoke from the factories
Poisoned our hillside
But ordinary people keep their pride and dignity.

Life on the East Side, life on the Eastside –
A place where the people know the people who know
  people just like you.

Ordinary Landmarks

Monday's always washing day – hope it doesn't rain.
Wednesday's when the bin man comes – every week
the same.
Friday night is bath night, tin baths by the fire.
All the ordinary landmarks in our lives.

Tuesday night he's out 'til late – dinner's getting cold.
Thursday Mam will take the kids – she's got a heart
of gold.
Church on Sunday morning – kids in Sunday best.
All the ordinary landmarks in our lives.

And so the years just keep flowing by,
People are born and they live and die.
A sea of faces that just pass you by.
And nothing seems to change.

Football on a Saturday – rain won't stop the play.
Chances missed and moments lost like every other day
As the small town people dream their lives away.
All the ordinary landmarks in our lives.

Soldier Secombe

Being a soldier meant we weren't afraid of audiences, because we'd faced bullets in action. No one's going to take a shot at you from the front row of the stalls ... although somebody did once ...but that's another story.

HARRY SECOMBE

While brother Fred made his way towards the ministry, Harry joined the Territorial Army as soon as he was legally able to do so. In fact he joined a year earlier than he was legally allowed to, but nobody asked any questions.

Promising good pay, an attractive uniform and trips abroad, the Territorials were seen as a good opportunity that any eighteen-year-old youth would be out of their mind to miss. The only snag was that a few months after Harry joined, World War Two was declared.

As Britain braced itself for instant bombing from the skies, Harry prepared himself for battle. The tense expectation gradually dissipated as the months of the 'phoney war' dragged on, and Harry was sent back home.

Continuing his job in the Colliery Department as junior
pay clerk for Baldwin's Ltd, Harry was eventually called
up to fight a few months later. By this time he had met a
man who was to become a lifelong pal.

'How can I forget the day I met Harry!' laughs Ray
Norwood. 'He was certainly a lively animal, always ready
to make a joke and have a laugh, but not to the point of
tedium. He was great fun to be with. We had joined the
Territorial Army in May 1939, and for some reason or
another we developed an affinity for one another on that
very day.'

Their friendship has lasted more than sixty years, and
was probably based not just on the fact that they were both
born in Swansea, but on a shared love of comedy. What got
them laughing before they even opened their mouths was
their comparative physical appearance. 'Harry was all
muscle and spectacles, and I was six foot one but only ten
stone. I was like a beanpole standing next to Harry,' laughs
Ray.

Had the comedy element developed seriously, one won-
ders if the pair would have beaten Little and Large to the
stage. There was little time for theatricalities, however, for
the days ahead held enough drama of their own.

While in the late thirties morality insisted that bare flesh
should be reserved only for the beach, the first thing the
new 'Reserve Terriers' had to endure was the medical.
Arriving at the old Swansea Barracks it was damp and
cold. Some of their comrades facing National Service plot-
ted all kinds of foils to try and avoid being called up. One
of these involved sucking on a large piece of soap that
would give the impression of foaming at the mouth.
Hopefully, if you could manage a little bit of serious
acting, the medical orderly would instantly recognize a
dreaded disease and send you home. Ray and Harry,

having volunteered for the Terriers, faced their ordeal with great courage.

'Having to strip down made us very self-conscious in this huge room, but seeing Harry standing there just beaming behind his large spectacles immediately raised my spirits. We queued up in a line with white faces and shivering bodies wondering whether we were awaiting emasculation. Suddenly this man in a white coat made a ferocious dash towards Harry's genitals and barked at him to cough. Going down the line and watching each man's privates must have been a very strange job, particularly when some of the boys behind us squealed and others were so shocked they meekly replied with a "Pardon?". "Cough! You wimpeys!" shouted the sergeant-major.'

The culture of the time made sure that each soldier was indeed shy, and when they found that their most treasured possession was under attack by a medical man it was a great shock to the system. It was not unknown for the doctor to use his wooden spatula to lift one man's organ for inspection, and use the same implement to hold the next man's tongue down.

The other act of torture on that particular day was the inoculation. 'We were told to line up standing sideways with our right hand by our sides. The orderly moved along the whole row filling the needle up and then sticking it in each arm as he went. By the time he arrived at the end of the row that point was like a knitting needle. I'm convinced that some of the screeching noises that came from that line found their way into *The Goon Show*.'

Ray was working for a ship-broking firm on Swansea Docks as a customs clerk. The customs officer was a colonel in the Royal Artillery. Harry's firm also contained workers who were connected with the Royal Artillery in Swansea. There was no real pressure to join the services at that time, but it was certainly seen as the right thing to do. At 11.15 a.m. on Sunday 3 September Neville Chamberlain, the British Prime Minister, announced to a nervous nation that Britain was now at war with Germany. Everybody held their breath, and Harry and Ray did the obvious thing and joined the Royal Artillery. They were now real soldiers.

Having signed all the necessary papers, they picked up their uniforms, the design of which still seemed more relevant to the First World War. The breeches and spurs, designed to help when riding a horse, were of no use to Ray and Harry, who walked back home feeling very self-conscious.

In fact, it seemed that most of the equipment had been resurrected from the last war too. Instead of arms, the battery of 250 men had pikes, and found themselves practising on 4.5 mm howitzer guns that were considered relics. Training took place two nights a week, with gun-laying and firing the order of the day. The young boys' delicate feet were not suited to army boots, as Ray recalls. 'For the first few months we got these huge blisters and sores on our feet and toes that constantly bled. It was pretty tough.'

The infamous army camp preceded four months of intensive training. 'Harry and I got really close, because we were literally living on top of each other in bell tents which seemed hopelessly unable to keep out any rain.'

Stationed in Malvern, Worcestershire, it was the first time that Ray noticed Harry's skill in mimicry. Fourteen shillings a week was the wage. Seven shillings went home to their families, which left them a shilling a day to spend. A packet of cigarettes would cost threepence, and a pint of beer sixpence. However, Ray found that by sticking with Harry you didn't actually need any money.

Like all good soldiers, upon arrival at Malvern their first reconnaissance mission was to the local pub. It was here that Harry sat down at the piano and went straight into a comedy routine that rocked the pub into laughter. Very soon the piano was covered with pints of beer donated by an admiring audience. Harry's tap dancing, monologues and singing provided the pair with enough beer to last several nights, particularly as they were not really drinkers. They were both just eighteen and all this alcohol was a foreign commodity.

Using an old coat, ruffling his hair and lifting a comb up to his lips, Harry finished his impromptu act with a parody of Adolf Hitler. It appealed to the sentiments of those watching, and brought the house down with cheers and hoots of pleasure. It was then that Ray began to realize that Harry was a special friend indeed!

'Harry was what I would describe as effervescent. Being with him was like opening a bottle of champagne with a "pop" and the bubbles keep going to the top. Harry was like that because you never saw him going "down" at all, he was always going to the top.'

Living in a bell tent with Harry could be either pure hell or pure heaven, depending on who you were and how acute your sense of humour was. He would keep most of his mates awake half the night in fits of laughter as he regaled them with imaginary plays about the day's proceedings, mimicking the officers in ridiculous situations. Either the sergeant major was deaf and didn't notice the noise or the convulsive shaking of the tent, or he was content for the boys to have their fun. Anyway, he got his own back during the day.

The food was foul. Stewed cabbage and half-cooked potatoes were almost unrecognizable as they were slopped on to the plates of the queuing soldiers. Any meat was to be found at the bottom of thin gravy with at least a half-inch of grease floating above it. Harry never complained,

29

he simply made a joke out of it, and tried not to think of the Blooms' farm back home.

They were well aware that the purpose of this two-week camp was to prepare them to kill people and yet the fact was continually pushed to the back of their minds. Confusion swam around Harry's head as he held a .303 rifle in his hands. His only dream was to make people laugh, not to shoot them dead or maim them. Perhaps he could make the enemy laugh himself to death? There were some in the camp who, having heard Harry's material, believed that this was highly possible!

Perhaps the fact that he was being trained to operate the artillery guns enabled him to realize that he would be shooting at a distance. Surely he would not actually see anybody killed as a result of his own action?

With the initial training over, the regiment came under full military discipline and was constantly moved from place to place as if part of a touring production. Uckfield, Carmarthen, Milburn Port and Aldershot were on the schedule, while they carried out routine duties and extended training. It was when they arrived in Scotland at the Firth of Forth that things really started to look serious. Out in the sea were several huge metal amphibious landing craft.

Once the men were on board, the craft sped out to sea, making a sudden U-turn in readiness for the practising of an invasion on to the beach. The weather was not good, and the craft were rocking from side to side with each wave that hit the ship. Several of those on board were immediately seasick, but there was little time for sympathy as the boats rolled swiftly towards the shore.

Harry and Ray's landing craft somehow managed to hit a sandbank and a large groan from the group of disappointed soldiers anxious to get on dry land echoed across the water. 'One of the officers in charge of the exercise came aboard,' explains Ray. 'He began to address us as we stood soaking wet, shivering and with no room to move. We felt like sardines in a tin. As the officer opened his mouth I suddenly heard a sheep bleating behind me. I couldn't believe it! How could a sheep have got on board with us? There wasn't room for a flea, let alone a sheep. The officer started to speak once more, and it happened again. "Baaa! Baaaa!" It caused every miserable soldier on board to break out into a broad smile. I looked behind me, and saw Harry with a big grin on his face.'

Back on dry land after a successful practice, Harry felt it was only a matter of time before they did it for real. They didn't know what, how or when, as everything was kept secret, but the sense of an impending task drew ever nearer. He didn't have to wait long. Although they didn't know it, on 15 October 1942 they were suddenly part of Operation Torch, the code name for the invasion of North Africa.

By this time the Wehrmacht was at its most forceful, the summer of 1942 marking the high point of German conquest. The offensive against Russia began well, but due to Hitler's over-adventurous ambition, and the fact that he frequently changed his mind and his plans, it soon lost momentum. At Stalingrad the mighty German army was halted, and the tide of war began to turn as severe winter conditions took their steady toll on the unprepared German infantry. Hitler's revered Sixth Army was trapped and over 300,000 died as a result. It was to be known as the coffin of German troops.

Meanwhile, several thousand miles away on a different fighting front, Harry was about to embark on an expedition that was to change the course of history and bring the end of the war another step closer. Operation Torch would begin with landings at Algiers, Oran and Casablanca on the north coast of Africa, and would bring victory in the desert against the infamous German commander, Rommel.

Harry's seaborne force was one of three and comprised 160 Royal Navy ships carrying 23,000 British troops and 10,000 Americans; it had acted as cover to the 250 Merchant Navy ships carrying forces from the Clyde. In total nearly three hundred ships carrying 100,000 men were part of an operation that had never been attempted on this scale before. It wasn't until the convoy of ships were well away from land that the troops had any idea where they were heading. Lance-Bombardier Secombe stared out to sea and visualized waving goodbye to his mother and father at Swansea station a few weeks previously, wondering how long it would be before he saw them again.

Now part of the 78th Division, they remained at sea for three weeks, zigzagging across the Atlantic in an effort to avoid the German U-boats that stalked the area in wolf packs. Arriving in the Mediterranean, it was 8 November when they were herded into the amphibious craft once more. Climbing down the green mesh that hung on the side of the boat, one by one they dropped into the metal assault craft.

The powerful motor glided them swiftly ashore. Avoiding any sandbanks this time, Harry was surprised and not a little relieved to notice a lack of enemy gunfire as they hit the beach. Unlike the Americans further down the coast who suffered some two thousand casualties, his battery received no injuries at all. The lack of resistance at Algiers was due to the fact that the rest of their regiment had already gone ahead two days before, in support of the invasion. Algiers was also poorly protected with the obsolete tanks and defence equipment used by the renegade French Vichy. Rather than confronting the feared enemy,

Ray and Harry were shocked when several Frenchwomen offering baskets of oranges met them instead. It all seemed so unreal.

Safely on dry land, they were even more surprised to hear that one of their ships had been struck by a torpedo and had gone down. It was, with hindsight, quite remarkable that, given the size of the convoy, they had not lost any more.

Once the beach-head had been secured, the regiment's first task was to assemble the guns that had followed them and advance inland and on up to Algiers, which had now itself been secured. The second objective was to capture the nearby Aerodrome, with some of the regiment being utilized as a support group to the main infantry. Ray was diverted to RHQ – the Regimental Headquarters, responsible for the logistics of the whole regiment and its action in the immediate area. This represented the hub of the battle, from where operation orders were issued.

Harry was sent to 321 Battery. There were three batteries to a regiment, each composed of eight 7.2 mm guns with a sergeant and six men assigned to operate each one. The smaller twenty-five-pounder guns worked alongside. Their main role was to shoot ahead of the infantry to destroy and weaken the enemy, and prepare the way for the advancing British troops.

The guns were pulled into position by motorized quads that also carried the gun crew. Behind the truck was the tender that carried the ammunition. The thought of a future Goon driving one of these hell-raisers is enough to make any reader's hair stand on end, but drive it Harry did.

Positioning the guns was an onerous task which sometimes required the digging of gun pits in order to secure them. It was when one of these guns with pneumatic wheels bounced out of its pit and over a cliff that Harry met a face that was to become very familiar in years to come. Gunner Milligan suddenly appeared inside Harry's wireless truck and said, 'Anybody seen a gun?'

If Secombe was surprised to meet Milligan, Milligan was just as surprised to meet Secombe. 'It was about this time that I saw something that I felt might put years on the war,' says Spike. 'It was a short gunner, wearing iron-frame spectacles, a steel helmet that obscured the top of his head, and baggy shorts that looked like a tea clipper under full sail. He was walking along a gulley behind a group of officers, heaped with equipment. It was my first sight of Gunner Secombe ... I never dreamed one day he, I, and a lone RAF clerk called Sellers, at that moment in Ceylon imagining he could hear tigers, would make a sort of comic history.'

During the occasional respite, Milligan and Harry were able to relax together in the war-torn, yet beautiful countryside. Spike remembers those occasions as moments of calm among the bombs. 'Ken Carter, who started Benny Hill off in the early TV days, played some of his own compositions. I think Harry Secombe sang, and Edgington played his piano as we sat on the balcony and enjoyed this divine night. The tranquillity has never left me in my life. Then we had to get back to the bloody war.' Later, they were to bump into each other again at the Central Pool of Artistes in Naples.

The regiment got its first taste of action when it fired its opening rounds of ammunition against the Germans on 17 November near Bône. Having assembled their equipment, survived a delayed but massive bombing campaign on the beach-head as they attempted to unload supplies, and marched five hundred miles north across mountains, they were granted a forty-eight-hour respite. It was not to last, and after a violent battle with exhausted soldiers the brigade was forced to abandon its attack on the town of Medjez-el-Bab.

During the fighting a battery commander was taken prisoner by the German paratroops and was their 'guest' for two days. Then, to his surprise and joy, they released him and he quickly rejoined his unit, who had recorded him as missing.

That night, German parachutists who had held the town withdrew after blowing the bridge across the Medjerda. The regiment advanced up the road to Tunis where Tobourba was found to be unoccupied, but were suddenly overrun by twenty-five enemy tanks. The battle lasted three hours, by which time fourteen tanks had been knocked out, but casualties on both sides were heavy. Among the fearsome array of weapons was a new type that used a very effective armour-piercing shell; the German tank crews were later forced to bolt extra metal plates on to the sides and front of their tanks in an attempt to withstand the mighty onslaught.

As the various battles progressed, the Royal Artillery's guns were used in astonishingly effective and brave close-range fighting of sometimes little more than a hundred yards. Although they were encouraged to fight together as batteries, the individual gun crews were also able to locate their own targets. On one occasion the Panzer divisions were lured into a trap, their chances of retreating virtually nil. At such close range the Royal Artillery was easily able to slaughter the German tanks, and in one attack alone, one individual gun was able to hit six enemy tanks with the first six rounds fired.

As the tanks advanced, they were then pounded with anything up to 150 Allied field guns, with the result that most of the Panzer divisions were swiftly annihilated. Without the support of the tanks the German infantry were able to do very little and piece by piece, over a matter of six months, more and more ground was reclaimed by the Allies. The German tanks destroyed by the Royal Artillery were seriously missed when Germany tried to defend the forthcoming onslaught on Tunisia itself.

Harry's role in battle was to maintain communications between the battery command post and the forward observation post, a tricky job which demanded the ability to dodge gunfire and shelling between the two! At the command post he assisted the officer in charge in plotting the range of the guns, ordering the ammunition and reporting on how the battle was going. All this took place as enemy shells flew almost constantly overhead.

Not all the fighting was successful. During one enemy tank attack eighteen guns and crew were lost in a devastating tank attack, and several other sections were almost surrounded by the enemy. It was a horrifying position to be in and one of the gunners was later awarded a Distinguished Conduct Medal for his bravery. Gallantry was a word that would often be repeated in later accounts of the struggle in the region.

The Royal Artillery worked alongside the infantry, a detachment of a dozen engineers and the Royal Signal Corps. Strong communication lines were essential on the battle front, and every time one of them was blown, a signaller had the unenviable task of repairing it, often under direct fire. The regiment's first casualty was a signaller. 'We'd come all the way along the first few miles of the North African coastline with little resistance,' remembers Ray. 'We were suddenly dive-bombed by German Stukas as we entered the battle of Tobourba, not far from our main objective, Tunis. We got into a field and then found we were under mortar fire coming down on top of us like rain. Our signaller, Eric, complained of being hit in the back with what turned out to be a piece of mortar shrapnel. We got him on a stretcher and he was sent off to hospital. We learnt later that he had died on the way, bringing the horror of war into reality. It really shook us.

'In the days before counselling was on offer, men who had lost friends and colleagues in the most appalling circumstances attempted to bite the traditional British stiff upper lip and simply carry on. None of us were heroes in the sense that we did desperate things. A man without fear can never really become a hero, it's the people who have fear and can overcome it that are the real heroes. Harry was always seemingly in the thick of the battle, covered in mud, and in this way just carried on with his duties.'

During bombardments the noise was unbearable and shook each man to the bone. Harry was recognized as a good soldier but amid the anxiety and terror of war, his sense of mischievousness and fun gave him an air of being more relaxed than most. In fact he was as terrified as the next man, and he had every right to be. They were in the middle of some of the most severe fighting of a war that would eventually clear the Axis forces out of North Africa.

Periods of rest could last anything from a few hours to several weeks, when the men's main duty would be patrolling. Harry's main duty seemed to be testing out the new voices he had acquired from the various officers and soldiers they lived with. It was Harry's mimicry that, according to Ray Norwood, created the most laughter, and in so doing literally helped keep them all sane. He could mimic anybody. 'Wherever Harry was it was lively, and wherever Harry was he made us laugh. I don't think people had time to get depressed when Harry was around, even if he was a bit down. One day I heard him telephone down the line and, in a perfect impersonation of a well-known officer's voice, order some wire. The poor subordinate at the other end obediently rushed to his stores and, grabbing the item required, ran to the officer he assumed had made the call. "I didn't order any wire, you twit!" retorted the surprised officer. Somehow avoiding near-lynching, Harry got away with it every single time. Each time he did, it made our lives a little bit more bearable.'

General Montgomery was unlike other generals in that he used to go and talk to the boys of war. A very 'show-bizzy' man, he would use his tank as a stage and confidently announce in his best clipped voice that they were going to beat the Germans, almost as if the result of the war had already been settled. After Montgomery had inspected the troops and left, Harry was free to gleefully place his glasses at an angle and on one side of his face, and mimic Montgomery's stern voice, much to the amusement of all around him.

For Harry, hearing his own laughter was important too. It was, he decided, when confronted with absolute terror, the best way to control his sphincter muscle! It was cathartic to laugh when death was all around, and in sight of him. One minute Harry would be chatting to a comrade, the next minute the man would be blown to pieces. Laughter was the only way to overcome such horrors.

Another one of Harry's alleged and infamous telephone conversations involved him answering the field phone to a young officer who believed he was the battery major. Assuming the voice of the major, he listened while the officer poured out his tale of woe. 'Sir! I've a brother up the line who I haven't been in touch with for some considerable time and I wondered if I could have a day or two off, so that I may see him?'

'Certainly, my man,' replied Harry with all the dignity of the major he was impersonating. The poor young officer took his time off but very soon found he was being charged for absence without leave. Fortunately for the officer, it was assumed that it had been confusing and difficult to hear on the battlefield, and he was eventually let off the charges. Harry has not been discovered to this day!

Great loyalty, and a firm sense that they were fighting for King and country, enabled Harry and his battery to survive the nine months of battle in North Africa before he found himself on board ship once again. This time he was heading across the Sicilian Channel in Operation Husky, along with two and a half thousand other ships.

On 10 July 1943, the island began to suffer colossal bombardment by the Royal Navy and operations soon began against a defending force of over 300,000 enemy troops. The teeming airfields of Tunisia supported the planes that bombed strategic targets and supplied the drop for the men and officers of the British First Air Landing Brigade and American paratroops.

After yet another beach landing, this time at Sousse, Harry's company spent the next few weeks slowly working their way up the difficult roads of the island, removing and capturing Germans as they advanced. Upon reaching the main German defence at Centuripe, they embarked on a fierce battle to dislodge the Germans that was to last several days. The massive bombardment that ensued was terrifying, and Harry found the explosive sound of the multiple mortars particularly shocking. Many of the men were reduced to wobbling jellies at the petrifying 'boom' an attack produced. Harry felt his own nerves were beginning to shatter.

As Spike Milligan was to record: 'There was great mortaring going on ahead and the road was blocked and there was flames and bullets and bombs that lit up the night sky so that you could have read a newspaper with no trouble. No, we didn't go there as conquerors, we arrived in Italy shit-scared and that is the truth.'

A comrade stumbled upon Harry one day squatting by a tiny stream known as a wadi. On closer inspection he noticed that Harry was washing a small white cloth, which seemed to sum up the whole situation. Harry was fed up with the war, he wanted to leave now, but if he was going to capitulate, then he would do it cleanly!

One of the favourite songs of the Eighth Army, in celebration of the fact that they had not been selected to take part in the catastrophic French invasion, was called 'The D-Day Dodgers', and was written by Hamish Henderson, one of the best poets from World War Two.

> We're the D-day dodgers out in Italy,
> Always on the vino, always on the spree,
> Eighth Army scroungers and our tanks
> We live in Rome among the Yanks,
> The happy D-day dodgers of sunny Italy.
>
> We landed at Salerno, a holiday with pay,
> The Jerries sent the bands out to greet us all the way,
> We all joined hands, they gave us tea,
> We all sang songs, the beer was free,
> The happy D-day dodgers of sunny Italy.

Other songs were more realistic, such as this one, sung to the tune of 'Lily Marlene':

> Look across the mountains
> In the wind and rain,
> See the wooden crosses,
> Some that bear no name.
> Heartbreak and toil
> And suffering gone,
> The lads beneath them

Slumber on,
The lucky D-day dodgers
Who'll stay in Italy.

As the regiments made their way up through the central mountains of Sicily, General Patton's US Army advanced on the northern, Palermo front while the Canadians moved in on the eastern, Catania side. The objective was Messina at the northernmost tip, which seems to touch the toe of Italy itself.

Although the Germans were in retreat, they put up strong resistance and it wasn't until 13 August that Harry and his companions consolidated with the US Army just north of Etna. 'We always had a bit of a laugh at the expense of the Yanks,' explains Ray. 'Their tank units were constantly making their way back through our advancing lines for repairs, and we used to joke that they were always on the retreat. One of the running gags we had going had a similar connotation and was about a British warship that pulled into harbour in America. An American soldier welcomes it with a booming "Hello guys! How's the second largest navy in the world?" The British sailor's riposte is "We're doin' fine. How's the second best?"'

Another wartime favourite involved the true story of an injured Polish pilot who was invited to regale a class at Roedean School in Sussex with his stories of daring and courage while in the air. 'One day I was flying and I looked behind me only to see these three German Fokkers right on my tail.'

The headmistress jumped up nervously to explain to the girls that 'Fokker' was a famous German aircraft manufacturer. 'You are quite right,' smiled the airman. 'Except that these Fokkers were Messerschmitts!'

The advancing Allied army contained not only Americans and Canadians but Indian, African and even

Jewish battalions. Of course it was all fodder for the Secombe send-up, which had obviously been spotted by an army talent scout, for suddenly Harry was drafted as a member of the Divisional Concert Party.

Ray was deeply saddened to leave his friend Gunner Secombe behind as he moved on to attack the famous Monte Cassino and then upwards into Austria. He hoped he might be able to see Harry again, but the fragility of life in war and the distance involved didn't offer him much hope. They shook hands and smiled bravely as they bid each other farewell.

Harry soon found others around him who shared his love of comedy and song, one of whom was comedian Norman Vaughan. Harry was impressed with Norman, whom he saw as a real professional, particularly when Norman, having seen Harry's act, asked him how long he had been in the business! It is quite ironic that a few years later it would be Harry who beat Norman to stardom.

Norman had himself been in the business almost from birth, having been born the son of a stage-struck father, and having started his career with a boys' troop called the Eton Boy Singers. They had nothing to do with Eton, but were twenty boy sopranos who wore high collars, and they had enjoyed a high degree of success. Norman was to teach Harry many techniques that he would soon put into practice in becoming more confident in front of an audience.

As a team they travelled around the captured Sicilian countryside entertaining military audiences from the back of a truck and feeling like true professionals. It was the perfect break for Harry, who could now rely on an audience that had the time to sit and listen rather than always being on the move. At last he could try out his material, learn essential comic timing and discover what really made people laugh. The Goons were on their way!

Sir Spike Milligan

The irrepressible Goon, Spike is a legend in his own lifetime, and still remembers Harry with a mixture of great affection and schoolboy naughtiness.

He's one of us. A first-generation comic. He doesn't give a pig's eye about all that grease-paint aristocracy. The only trouble is, I should warn you, he is quite mad.

Harry Secombe is funny, like a dervish. I'm always waiting for him to break something. Filled with raspberries and all sorts of double-meaning noises. And of course he's very British. Now that is an impossible thing to be unless, maybe, we're collectively fighting some other country like Germany. Otherwise we are English or Irish or Scots or Welsh. Harry manages to be very pro-British – nearly anti-Welsh. Do you know that he doesn't even go to rugby matches?

And when I was talking about Plaid Cymru and praising them, Harry came on very strongly against them. But he has this great love of people: when I went to his house-warming party nearly everybody who was anybody was there, but he made straight for me. He has this affection for me.

Jimmy Young

Having been in show business for longer than he cares to remember, and now in his seventies, Jimmy Young remains one of the key elements in the success of BBC Radio 2's daytime broadcasting. It's obvious that Jimmy's millions of listeners love him dearly.

Sadly, I have never had the pleasure of working with Harry and have only met him on social occasions. Having said that, he has the extraordinary ability to make you feel, even on those occasional meetings, as though you had always been the closest of friends.

His show business career is, of course, legendary. The Goons, the shaving sketch, the stories are endless. Not only is he a genuinely funny man, on stage and off, he combines a high comic talent with a singing career which would be sufficient satisfaction for most artists on its own.

Ken Williams

An ardent fan for more than fifty years, Ken grew up with the Goons and says that they were comic heroes to him and his peers. Even in recalling their escapades of so long ago, the memory is fresh and Ken easily breaks into laughter as it all comes back to mind.

The Goons storylines were based on different aspects of the Second World War which we had all just emerged from, and so we were glad to reflect on those dark days with some laughter. I suppose it was a sort of therapy, but the main reason for its popularity was in knowing the background to the war and therefore being able to appreciate the jokes.

One of the episodes is set in England during the war when one of the characters lights a match and hears a bang as the German guns fire at them. He then decides to light a German match in the hope of being spared, but the English guns start firing at them. They really took the mickey out of the war.

Harry, playing Neddy Seagoon, came across as the big fat simple one. He was not as stupid as Eccles and Bluebottle, of course! They were really, really thick, and the cause of much hilarity. Seagoon's was the main character thread that ran through the series, and storylines tended to revolve around him, so Harry mainly concentrated on playing this one character. Peter Sellers played Major Dennis Bloodnok and was like a Colonel Blimp, the archetypal army officer, and they would spend their time trying to con Seagoon into all manner of stupid escapades.

The combination of their talents was simply wonderful. With Spike writing the scripts, Peter doing a hundred voices, and Harry acting as a sort of anchor, it couldn't have been better for the ordinary listener like me. Ray Ellington, Max Geldray on the harmonica, conductor Wally Stott, and announcer Wallace Greenslade were often unexpectedly pulled into the action when they weren't looking. Although intended as an adult programme, I noticed that kids loved it too, for behind the stupidity there was another layer.

All sort of things would trigger one of Seagoon's raspberries, sometimes just as part of a conversation, instead of a word. It was so anarchic and off the wall that a simple raspberry would cause everyone to roll around on the floor. Unlike a lot of comedy today which produces titters with the occasional hoot, the Goons were a belly laugh from beginning to end. Sometimes it was quite exhausting listening to them, and I emerged from the programme literally with aching sides. The programme brought so many others and me such pleasure, so much so that I would always make a point of not going out the night it was broadcast. All my work colleagues would rush home on a Tuesday to make sure we were ready when the programme started. None of us wanted to miss an episode and it was the main topic of conversation at the work the following day. Any evening meetings at the bank I worked in would have been carefully planned to avoid a clash!

Before the Goons, a comedian on the radio really just told a joke. ITMA was on during the war, but again its comedy was very 'sensible'. The Goons changed all that, indeed they changed the face of comedy for all time.

When someone today thinks of John Cleese they recall *Fawlty Towers*. In the same way, when someone mentions Harry Secombe to me, I think of the Goons. If Harry were to walk in the room now, I would not be able to say anything, I would be laughing too much!

Peter Goodwright

Peter's career as a comedian in broadcasting, live theatre and most recently the cruise ships, has spanned more than thirty-five years, but it began in a similar way to Harry's.

In 1955, Her Majesty's Government was kind enough to invite me to join the Royal Air Force. As I thought it would be churlish to refuse, not to mention unpatriotic and disloyal – plus the fact that they might send a hit squad to come and get me if I didn't go – I went along and underwent what was known as 'basic training'. This operation took place at RAF Hednesford in the wintertime, and was the nearest I'd been to hell since failing O-level Latin.

The memory of the constantly falling icy rain, the muddy fields, the rock-hard beds, the polishing, the cleaning, the drill instructors, the shouting, the marching up and down, the five-mile run with full kit, the cold showers and the general misery which is the lot of 'basic trainers' is with me still.

So too is the one bright spot in this miserable charade. Harry Secombe, the arch-Goon, was to appear at the camp theatre. There were no bookable seats – if you wanted to be there, you queued in the rain. This I did, and was rewarded with an unforgettable experience. Harry was explosively funny and filled the small theatre with a great magic. And as if the comedy was not enough – he sang to us.

The silence of my fellow conscripts, listening to the music, was in such sharp contrast to the noise and harsh living which we endured in the outside world, that it left an indelible impression on me. Such cheers and applause when the show was over – and quite rightly too!

I don't suppose Harry even remembers this event, but I do. It restored my faith in human nature, and gave me cause to thank God for the great talent he gave to that Neddy Seagoon – what, what, what, what!

Dame Vera Lynn

The original 'Forces' Sweetheart' kept hearts and spirits alive both during and after the war with her wonderful voice, beautiful figure and bubbling personality.

Harry was at the bottom of the bill when I first met him in 1950. We were both appearing in the same show in Blackpool, and he was a terrifically funny man to be around. It was a wonderful summer season, and one that I'll not easily forget. There were so many performers coming out of the army, including my brother who did a double act with a young Max Bygraves. Harry was special somehow, and it was pretty obvious that he would blossom quickly, and I'm glad he did.

Years later, when we were planning for the 50th Anniversary of VE day celebrations outside Buckingham Palace I suggested Harry to the organiser Michael Parker. We needed someone who was younger and could appeal to a broad section of the public, as well as someone who was actually in the army. I suggested Cliff and Harry Secombe! Fortunately, both the boys were available, and proved to be the perfect choice for a memorable occasion. The public and the Palace were certainly amused!

On that day, Harry worked like he always did, and gave one hundred percent of his personality. Harry is one of the biggest hearted people in show business, and I cannot think of anyone more loved.

Lin Bennett

Larger-than-life comedian and singer Lin pays tribute to the man he says started it all.

Being asked to write a brief account of my feelings about the wonderful Sir Harry Secombe is a bit like being asked to read *War and Peace* in a day – it can't be done!

My introduction to this great man came as I grew up in the fifties and sixties. I remember hearing this really funny programme on the radio called *The Goon Show*. After just one episode, I rearranged my whole schedule so that I wouldn't miss a single show. I was captivated, spellbound.

From my little transistor radio these men were coming out with the daftest story lines imaginable, they were fooling around in front of a microphone, they were being silly, acting like clowns – but they were making me laugh till I cried.

So I saved my pennies until I had enough to buy myself a tape recorder, and recorded all the shows – one after another. Oh, if only I had kept those tapes!! I didn't realize it then, but this was radical radio in the making. It was different, very different.

My favourite character in the Goons was Neddy Seagoon, who was played by Harry. I even got to play his part in a display put on by the Boys' Brigade somewhere around 1959 – and I can still remember many of the lines to this day!

With a developing bubbly personality of my own, I related very much to Harry and he quickly became my mentor. I mimicked his mannerisms, his giggle, his laugh and his great sense of fun. I loved the way he used his facial movements, especially his eyebrows, to get a laugh. He seemed to take nothing seriously. Everything and everyone was fair game to his zany sense of humour – whether they liked it or not.

But there was more to Harry than first met the eye. There was a serious side to this highly talented man, a side you didn't often see, but it was there all the same. You saw it when he sang. When you heard that wonderful velvet voice, he was showing another side of his talent. His humour and his songs appealed to me enormously.

Even at such a young age I met people who seemed to take life far too seriously – if Harry could make them laugh, and sing to them, then as sure as eggs are eggs, so could I. And I did, and I still do. Much, if not all of this, I directly attribute to Sir Harry.

Chris Libretto

The latest member of Harry's fan club once caused an
accident which he attributes to Harry.

As a lifelong fan of Harry, I remember walking down the high street one day, practising the silly faces that were his forte. Occasionally I would glance at my reflection in a shop window as I passed. Pleased with the result, I was instantly spurred on to twist my face as grotesquely as possible in a vain attempt to emulate Harry. Having reached the limits of facial contortion, I stopped to admire the reflection in a butcher's, looking like something out of a horror movie. Suddenly an elderly lady walked out of the shop doorway and dropped her bag of sausages with a scream of utter surprise. I walked away with what I call a 'Harry's grin' on my face.

Shaving Secombe

Every comic needs a disaster, it makes you more streetwise.

HARRY SECOMBE

'Is it possible to have a vocation as a comedian?' Harry cautiously enquired of his brother Fred as they walked around Swansea's Singleton Park together. 'Of course it's perfectly possible,' affirmed the newly assigned curate. Fred went on to assure him that his parents would also be thrilled, probably because Harry would be joining a profession they would dearly have loved to be part of themselves.

Having spent four years actively fighting the enemy in some of the most hazardous situations on earth, Gunner Secombe had now returned to Civvy Street. The time he had spent with the Divisional Concert Party had enabled a dream to come true, but could the dream really live on back in Blighty? Despite spending five weeks in a military hospital in Italy suffering from an inflammation of the gall bladder and kidneys, Harry looked back over the last few months of the war with deep gratitude. He had left many of his friends and comrades lying under the ground while he had survived, but he had also discovered the ability to make a real audience laugh, and had cherished every opportunity.

The garrison theatres were dotted all over the battlefields, and when he wasn't performing from the back of an army truck, this is where he would be found. A notice outside an old cinema requesting volunteers to entertain the troops was readily snapped up by Harry and he soon found himself a member of a semi-professional concert party. From army trucks and old theatres Harry's shows progressed to a kind of travelling circus touring across Italy with their own marquee, and setting up wherever they could. Like many comics, Harry began as an impressionist before creating an amalgam of everything he had seen or heard. Eventually a style of his own developed as they toured the camps.

These regular concerts finally convinced Harry that he should seek work in the entertainment business when he eventually got back home. But how on earth could it be done? It was meeting Myra that was to change the course of history and encourage him to fulfil his dream.

The Mumbles electric train ran along the coastline of South Wales from the lighthouse to Swansea, and past the Pier Hotel. The dance hall in the hotel was famous for its comfortable musical atmosphere and was always packed with young demobs looking for relaxation and fun. It was here that Harry first set eyes on a beautiful dark-eyed girl who accepted his confident invitation to dance.

The rest of that summer was spent in each other's company, often taking picnics down to the beautiful beaches, strolling along the cliffs, and seeing shows at the Swansea Empire. This venue became a regular meeting place as both shared a love of the old theatre, which quickly transported them from a land restoring itself after a war, into the never-never land of show business. Before you even glanced at the stage, however, this ornate Victorian theatre provided unique characters of its own.

Mr Penny was the proud doorman. He always stood to greet the public in an immaculate uniform of shiny peaked cap, gold stripes and braid as they queued to see the latest production. Each evening, all the staff would line up for his inspection, in which even hands and fingernails were checked for cleanliness. Mr Penny's big white gloves shone as he stood shouting out his soliloquy down the line: 'Sorry, ladies and gentlemen, there are no seats tonight. There are no seats tonight.' It was said that if you slipped something into the white gloves an extra seat or two would probably be found!

Harry Holmes, the night-watchman, was quite a character too. He had been an unicyclist going by the name of Cyclino. Known locally as the first man to cross the water from Mumbles Pier to Porthcawl on a floating pedal cycle, he now stayed in the theatre all night for security purposes.

It was an established practice for many of the local boys to pop round to the stage door after a show in order to meet the chorus girls and it was sometimes possible to fix up a date in this way. But Harry already had his date, and as they sat together watching all manner of plays, variety shows and musicals Harry felt the tug in his heart grow stronger. How would he ever be able to dance, sing and perform like these people in this quintessential venue? Although Harry was totally unaware of the part that the Empire would play in his own life, he was certainly aware of its proud history.

For almost seventy years, the Empire Theatre in Swansea was one of the major centres of entertainment. The Pavilion, as the theatre had previously been named, was bought in the 1890s by the legendary H.E. Moss, father of the Moss

Empires, and Oswald Stoll, and after redecoration, it opened as the Empire.

Everything was done in style, and there were performances twice nightly. The local press advertised that 'The ascent of a flight of rockets from the roof (wet nights excepted) will denote that the first performance is over.'

The bill on the opening night of the Empire, as advertised in the local press, was certainly impressive: 'Leoni Clark – and a troupe of 170 trained cats, mice, rabbits and canaries. Mr George Robey, character comedian; Hassan, the great American acrobat; Mary Clark, ballad vocalist; Tracey and Clark, patterers, singers and dancers and Kate Harvey, Queen of serio-comedy.' The Empire was soon to enjoy visits from hundreds of big-name stars, from Marie Lloyd to Max Miller and Sir Harry Lauder.

It wasn't long before the theatre became so popular that it could no longer accommodate the large, twice-nightly audiences and by Christmas 1900, a new and bigger Empire Theatre was being built in Oxford Street. It cost forty thousand pounds and was considered to be one of the finest theatres outside London. Despite the luxury of the new Empire, the prices of the seats on that opening week covered a range that nearly everyone could afford.

On one occasion the Morriston Male Voice Choir was invited to sing at every performance for a week. The deacons of the Morriston Chapels strongly objected and threatened to excommunicate the members of the choir if they performed on the Sunday. A great controversy ensued, but the concert went ahead.

Another member of the church who was not afraid to work on a Sunday was General Booth, founder of the Salvation Army. On Sunday 12 February 1911 General Booth graced the stage and lectured on 'The Salvation Army: what it is; what it does; and what it is destined to do'.

Some may consider that the opposition played the same stage. Houdini himself appeared at the theatre in 1911. A local newspaper of the time reported: 'Truly thrilling is the performance of Houdini at the Swansea Empire this week. He accomplished two or three feats last night which were positively marvellous, and made it abundantly clear that he entertained no fear of any locks, bolts, or bars which fly asunder with the most astounding rapidity – no matter how intricate or ingenious their construction.'

On the Wednesday of that week, the following letter appeared in the *Daily Post*:

> *We, the undersigned, Carpenters, hereby challenge you to escape from a packing case which we will construct out of rough heavy timber, into which we will so nail and rope you that it will be impossible for you to escape. Christopher Hodge, builder and contractor, 13 Hanover Street, Swansea; John Goodwin, 15 Courteney Street, Manselton and Benjamin B. Davies, 39 Vincent Street, Employees of T.W. Thomas and Co, Ltd.*

Houdini took the bait:

> *Houdini accepts the challenge under the condition that the box is not air tight. He agrees to forfeit £25 to anyone who can find any concealed instruments on him when he enters the box. He will make the attempt, second performance, Swansea Empire, Friday, May 5th, 1911.*

Saturday's newspaper records:

Houdini, the handcuff king and jail-breaker, surprised a record Friday night's audience at the Swansea Empire by getting out of a wooden box made by quali-fied Swansea carpenters, in which he was shut up and nailed in and strapped around. The large audience cheered him to the echo as he made his appearance out of the cabinet apparently cool and without showing he had moved an hair.

While Harry was fighting in Algiers, the heavy bombing of Swansea town during World War Two forced the manage-ment to change the performance times from 6 and 8.30 to 3.15 and 6 p.m. so that the shows would be over before the raids began. Three nights of terror bombing in February 1941 left the centre of Swansea devastated and burning. However, the theatre escaped unscathed and it was business as usual, even though many of the acts were reluctant to appear. On the night of the 21st, however, a bomb landed nearby. The theatre's roof was destroyed in the resulting fire and the Empire was forced to close for three months while a new roof was built. Most of the fit and able men had gone away to the war and women did much of the backstage work.

As the war dragged on, there were great changes at the Empire. In 1943, the first large-scale pantomime came. It was a production of *Aladdin* that ran for five and a half weeks. Long-running pantos then became the norm. *Goody Two Shoes* ran for 102 performances and starred Morecambe and Wise as the town councillors.

However, the longest-running pantomime of all was to be *Puss in Boots*, starring none other than local boy Harry Secombe. The show was extended to 116 performances, from 24 December 1952 to 14 March 1953. It had taken Harry less than seven years to swap his seat in the auditorium for the top of the bill and centre stage.

Not long afterwards the advent of television heralded the end of the age of variety and many theatres came under serious threat of closure. Manager Gwyn Rees sensed that the Swansea Empire's days were numbered. It was decided that the pantomime of 1957 was to be the last. After the curtain fell on 18 February in that year, the Empire would be no more.

Jack and the Beanstalk featured Welsh star names, Ossie Morris and Wyn Calvin, and on the last night, there was a black market for tickets, while the backstage atmosphere was simply electric. At the end of the performance, Mayor Harry Libby stepped from the wings on to the stage to bid goodbye to the Empire on behalf of the people of Swansea. The theatre chaplain came on to the stage to pray and chief commissionaire Alf Penny, proudly wearing his uniform, looked on at the death of his beloved Empire. Shortly afterwards the well-loved theatre that had inspired so many entertainers was flattened.

For Harry, those sixty-eight months between reading the programme and having his name printed in it were to be filled with all manner of shows and concerts, but before that he had to overcome the terror of his first audition.

Having just arrived home from the war, he had received a wonderful welcome from the family, who had handed him the letter which contained an offer to resume his old job at Baldwin's. But he felt so far removed from his old life that it would simply be impossible to go back to where he had come from. He had moved on so far, with new experiences and a delicious taste of show business, that going back to his old job would be like a betrayal of all he had been through. Harry politely turned the kind offer down and encouraged by his parents, Fred, Carol and above all, Myra, he finally set his sights on the big city.

If there's one thing that Harry Secombe will never forget, it's the day he auditioned for a spot at the famous Windmill Theatre. Having never been drawn into heavy drinking or smoking as an antidote to severe nerves, he was severely tempted to do so as he paced anxiously backwards and forwards in the street outside the theatre in London's Soho.

Infamous for its use of nude girls, the Windmill Theatre, run by impresario Vivian Van Damm, was an extremely popular attraction. Responsibility for public decency at that time was in the hands of the Lord Chamberlain's Office. This ruled that the models would be allowed to appear naked if they didn't move. As Harry was later to comment, 'The girls only wore three beads, and two of those were perspiration!'

In fact the three or four scenes that included the nudes were carefully choreographed, and it was all very decorous. Many of the girls were surprisingly prudish and required their colleagues to go into the auditorium to check that their pose was decent. Sitting first up in the 'gods', then in the dress circle, then in the stalls, each view of the girls was carefully analysed, and meticulously kept throughout the run of a few months. Despite its dubious reputation, the theatre had very high standards.

Harry's family were eager and expectant for their son to get the job. They realized how important the business was becoming to Harry and felt it was time he got his foot on the ladder. When Harry arrived backstage, ready to display his skill, he was surprised at how crowded it was. Another young hopeful, Norman Wisdom, bumped into him: 'Among the various places in which I sought work was the famous Windmill Theatre. Vivian Van Damm had advertised for acts and so I went along for an audition. I had only done a few minutes of my act when he waved me aside and called "Next!"

'He did thank me for attending but that was it – I was a failure, and not a successful one either. There was another young man auditioning on that same day and he was given a booking. In those days, no one had ever heard of the man who was to become *Sir* Harry Secombe.

'He was a nice chap even then and he commiserated with me in my failure. "Never mind mate, you'll make it!" he said.'

Harry's words of encouragement proved to be right, not just for Norman, but for himself too as he launched into a comical shaving act which was soon to become famous. Harry had developed this simple but effective routine, in which he demonstrated the different ways various men have of shaving, while racking his brain for new material for the army shows.

It was a unique sketch, but Harry expected to hear the familiar shout of 'Next!' bellowed across the footlights. Instead he was asked to come to the manager's office where, to his surprise and delight, he was offered a gruelling six-week run of thirty-six performances every week. There were six shows a day.

At the performance, the band played and the curtains were lifted, and the beautiful tableau of naked statues tried not to quiver in front of a gawping and constantly full house of excited men. After a few minutes of music the curtain would be lowered and on would dash a comic, a singer or a juggler while backstage the statues changed costume and position ready for the next montage. The comic would try and get a laugh in the six minutes or so he had available to him, the singer would exit, hopefully with some applause, and the juggler would try not to drop his clubs.

With Van Damm's eye for comedy talent, it was a marvellous experience and showcase for any aspiring performer.

The audiences were fairly rowdy and would fight to get into the front row between tableaus, and so Harry quickly learnt the art of 'grabbing' an audience.

He may have won the job, but the pay certainly didn't mean much. The twenty pounds a week he earned was far from a fortune, but for the time being at least he could afford food and comfortable lodgings in Kilburn, north London.

Each member of the family travelled to London to proudly watch Harry in his first professional show. Reverend Secombe attended, sensibly without dog collar. Had he forgotten to remove it just before entering the theatre, it would no doubt have raised more than a few eyebrows. 'His singing and shaving act was the most memorable part of his performance,' remembers Fred. 'Mind you, the meal we shared with Spike Milligan after the show was pretty good too!'

Harry had recently met Spike again, and was now sharing a flat with him and Norman Vaughan. If Harry had a bad side to his character at all, it was that if Milligan suffered from an untidy brain, Harry was able to emulate this physically by reducing a room to a chaotic clutter. Spike, used to living in a very orderly home with his mother, complained that Harry was an expert at creating chaos. He even joked that when Harry was discharged from the army's CPO, they burnt the hospital down for safety.

'Number 13 Linden Gardens in London's Notting Hill Gate will always have vivid memories for me,' remembers Norman. 'If there was one person in the whole world who didn't like Harry Secombe it was our landlady Blanche. She had the job of cleaning up after us but got fed up with picking up his empty Brylcreem bottles from all over the floor. I was the tidy one and Harry was the slob. Blanche used to come in flicking her cigarette ash into the pocket of her apron and shout "Has that Larry Felcombe been here again?!"'

Off stage, their social life was important and it was Michael Bentine, also working at the Windmill, who introduced Harry to a pub where they were served after hours. Like most of the public, performers tend not to go straight to bed after a day's work, even if that day's work finishes at 11 p.m. For most of the performers coming out of the theatres of London there were few choices, but Jimmy Grafton's pub was one of them.

An ex-major, Jimmy was sympathetic to the likes of Harry and Michael, who soon became regulars and friends. They soon discovered that Jimmy was writing comedy material for other comedians, and their combined love of the art brought about impromptu sketches which stretched late into the night and early mornings.

It was here that Spike Milligan, Michael Bentine, Peter Sellers and Harry Secombe first met as a foursome. Little did they know what their initial drink together would generate for the future. This was the birthplace of the Goons – but plenty of hungry unemployment was to come first.

Another budding comedian who nearly became a Goon was Henry Leslie. As variety fan Art Deane recalls: 'Better known as Les Henry, he started playing harmonica in 1928, and got his first chromatic in 1934 after seeing Larry Adler at the local cinema. He had an offer to go on tour with Brian Michie's Radio Stars of 1939, a job which he took and earned three pounds five shillings per week. When another agent offered him four pounds five shillings he took the job and stayed with that show until 1941 when he was called up.

'He became a dispatch rider, going through the North Africa campaign, Italy and Austria. The last six months were spent in Naples with Combined Services Entertainments, where he met Harry, Spike, and Norman Vaughan.

He joined the team as they took their show to the troops in Italy, Greece and Malta, finishing up at the Berger Theatre in Vienna.

'Once out of the services they used to gather in a place called Annie's Café in Windmill Street; it was there that Harry and Spike said to him, "We're going to try and do a show on the radio, why don't you join us? You could do your funny voice and play the harmonica." As he had also been approached by two other blokes to form a harmonica trio, he joined them. If he had gone with Harry and Spike his voice may have been used instead of Peter Sellers and perhaps his harmonica heard instead of Max Geldray. Isn't it a funny world?'

Les went on to be part of one of the most popular speciality comedy acts of the day, The Monarchs, who were formed in 1946. Their first show was at Fisher's Restaurant in London. They were waiting to go on when suddenly the agent said, 'What are you going to call yourselves?' Les suddenly called 'The Monarchs, the Kings of the Harmonica'. Les must have had a way with words because it was he who invented the phrase 'Harmonically Yours', which he used when signing autographs. They toured in more than thirty countries, and joined a host of stars at the London Palladium including Des O'Connor, The Bachelors and the fabulous Lena Horne. Almost twenty years have passed since their retirement, yet The Monarchs are still remembered by a large band of enthusiasts all over the world.

Harry encouraged Les in finding work and refining his act, and that year Harry spent Christmas back at home, giving him the chance to spend more precious moments with Myra. It didn't stop him worrying about the future, though, and whether another job would ever come along. Yet it did; Harry was thrilled to be offered a tour in

Germany with a Combined Services Entertainments show early in the New Year. Myra was to get used to waving Harry off, but this time he used his earnings on the tour to save for an engagement ring.

Arriving back home, he bought the ring they had chosen in a jeweller's shop in Swansea, and with the wholehearted blessing of the family prepared for the big day. In fact there was to be a royal wedding the same year, as Harry himself recalls in an interview with *TV Times*: 'We had the day off to watch the Royal Wedding on black and white TV and lots of relatives came round to join us. It was a great occasion. Clothes rationing was still in force and although Buckingham Palace had said the ceremony was not to be extravagant, I remember thinking how beautiful Princess Elizabeth looked and how dashing Prince Philip was. The wedding was a marvellous thing to see and very welcome at that time. We married three months afterwards in Swansea.'

Harry and Myra's own 'Royal Wedding' took place on 19 February 1948 with Rev. Fred Secombe taking the ceremony. 'When I stood with them in front of the altar and asked Harry to place the ring on Myra's hand I wondered if the classic tale of the lost ring would come true. The problem on this day was that due to Harry's nervousness he inadvertently placed the ring on the wrong finger. "Not that one, the other one!" I cried.'

St. Barnabas, Swansea, was the same parish church in which Fred had been married. This time the organist was none other than the resident musician at the Windmill Theatre. Used to playing as women undressed, he proudly struck the notes that were making history for two lovers in love. At the end of the traditional service he somehow wove 'I'm just wild about Harry, and Harry's wild about me' into the Toccata and Fugue in D minor as they exited down the aisle.

'Every man needs a cushion to lean on and Harry had Myra,' a wedding guest explained. 'Every man needs to have comfort, and comfort is not just an easy chair, it's relationships. I would go as far as to say that Harry's meeting of Myra was a result of divine intervention. One of the greatest things on earth was when Harry married Myra. I reckon that Myra is one of the shining stars of Harry's stardom.'

It was to be no ordinary marriage, but a very successful and happy relationship that has lasted for many, many years.

After a romantic honeymoon in Penzance, Harry was suddenly offered a part in a show in which all the cast wore women's clothes. The young Danny La Rue was one of them.

'*Forces Showboat* was an extremely popular post-war revue and made fortunes for the producers,' explains Danny. 'We could spend months playing the London theatres because there were so many of them, particularly the Empire circuit. I was a very quiet young lad, but had already started to master the art of female impersonation, and in 1949 one newspaper reviewer questioned why, in an all-male show, there should be that very attractive young lady!

'We had what was called a "train call" where we had to be at the station at a particular time to travel on the same train as the scenery. We got our tickets free of charge on those occasions. Harry and I would chat away for hours as we sped from one side of the country to the other. Having been a window dresser, I made all my own costumes, and Harry would watch in awe as all the other boys constantly sat sewing sequins on to their dresses. It was all very camp, and we were like a troop of chorus girls.'

On another show, the theatre management were unable to pay Harry and Danny their wages. Performers didn't really have a 'voice' in those days, for Equity only dealt with proper actors. The union only started to represent variety performers in 1968 when it amalgamated with the Variety Artistes Federation, but since Danny and Harry couldn't afford to be members of that organization, they just had to take non-payment on the nose. It hurt too!

'We were snowbound in Bristol in the middle of January and couldn't afford to get on the train. Harry's brother Fred had been to see the show and gave us the money we needed to get back home, with a bit left over for some food. It was very generous of him.'

Further tours and shows were offered which kept the young married couple from starvation, though it often seemed salvation came only at the last minute. One tour with Norman Vaughan arrived at the Grand Theatre in Bolton, where Harry presented his usual sketch.

'Sorry folks!' Harry announced as he rushed on to the stage with a table, a shaving brush, a mug and a razor. 'I've only just got here so if you don't mind, I'll have a shave first!' Something was awry in the auditorium and the audience didn't get the joke. One member was heard to ask afterwards whether the young comic would mind preparing himself properly before he arrived at the theatre next time! After a sharp discussion with this individual, Harry was horrified to discover that he was none other than the manager of the theatre. 'I couldn't believe it when Harry was paid off by the manager,' says Norman Vaughan. 'Somehow this guy really thought Harry was shaving for real!'

Sundays were rarely seen as days off; every chance for work had to be taken. One such opportunity produced a sequence of one-off radio broadcasts and a trial series with the BBC. Myra and Harry decided to move to London, since that would surely give Harry a better opportunity to find work, and they began their exile from Wales in rented premises in Brixton. Myra was soon expecting their first child and Harry was all too aware of the growing urgency for regular work.

New Year's Day in 1949 was Harry's first live television broadcast, from the BBC's Alexandra Palace studios in North London. Instead of the shaving sketch, Harry offered a similar tale of how different people eat their sand-wiches. It was an adventurous idea that resulted in him spitting mouthfuls of bread everywhere, but he didn't know whether it was actually funny or not. Fortunately the rehearsed and the ad-libbed material seemed to please both producer and audience.

Harry was fast becoming known as a radio and stage comic who gave good value, and shortly afterwards he was invited to appear in top comedian Cyril Fletcher's summer show, as well as making several appearances with him in his television show. It was just what Harry and Myra had prayed for as they prepared for the arrival of their child.

It was quite an eventful season, as Cyril himself recalls.

Our third year at Torquay, we had among a strong cast an unknown called Harry Secombe. He had not as yet acquired the stardom of The Goon Show. *He had been on a variety bill with me at Grimsby (I only played the number ones!!) and I had greatly enjoyed his unusual act. This consisted of his comedy shaving and finished with a soprano and tenor duet in which he himself did both characters, and I asked him if he would like to join us for the summer. He was keen to do it as he had a family on the way, and twelve weeks at the seaside was an attractive proposition. I explained to him that I wanted Betty to see his perfor-mance before we decided finally to book him, and it was arranged that Betty should see him at the Hippodrome, Eastbourne, where he was appearing – so oddly for Harry – in an all-male drag-show revue. In this show, incidentally, and looking exactly and equally as beautiful as Kim Kendall, was, aged about twenty, an exotic performer called Danny La Rue. 'That one is going to be a star,' said Betty.*

Now I must explain here that we had started to breed and show cocker spaniels with a small amount of success and one of our puppies had been bought by a couple at Brighton. 'We will take the puppy to Brighton,' I said, 'and then go on to Eastbourne and see Harry Secombe.' This we did. It was also the first puppy we had ever sold. He was beautiful and loving and I knew that parting with him was going to be difficult for Betty. The deal was made, the new owners approved of and we were about to go. As we said goodbye the puppy looked back at Betty in a way only a cocker spaniel can look back, and Betty, in the car on the way to Eastbourne, was in tears. As we sat in the circle of the Hippodrome watching Harry Secombe, Betty was still in tears; half for the disposed-of spaniel and half tears of laughter at Harry. It says a lot for Harry's marvellous gift of comedy even in those early days that he could exact tears of laughter from Betty under these circumstances. Next day we bought the spaniel back and signed up Harry Secombe for the summer.

He was a joy to have in the show. He was so funny, so ebullient and so undisciplined. On one occasion we were doing a sketch where Betty and Harry and I were drinking tea together. Things got so out of hand between Harry and Betty that Betty was eventually pouring tea out of the teapot over Harry's head and he was enjoying it enormously, as if he were under a shower in the bathroom. One of the stagehands was a fisherman who used to peddle the most delicious prawns to the company. Harry would go on in a serious scene (a serious scene with Secombe!) with the odd prawn or two palmed so that the audience could not see it, and as he danced a gavotte (he was slimmer then!) with Betty, she would find herself left holding a prawn, and this prawn would go round the whole of the company playing the scene quite unknown to the audience, who were possibly wondering why they all looked so happy up there on the stage!

Harry's whole concept of humour was original and a little before its time. The audience, not having yet been geared to the zany humour of the Goons, was a little unsure whether Harry was funny or not. A lot of them thought so. No one thought he was funnier than did Betty and I, who used to watch him with great delight from the wings. He never got enough applause for his funniest efforts, and knowing what a good tenor voice he had, we tried for several weeks to persuade him to finish on a serious song. 'No,' he said, 'I am a comedian.' 'But you are a singer, too,' we told him, and eventually we prevailed. The result of all this was that he was to become one of Britain's greatest and most lovable stars.'

If Cyril and Betty had told Harry this, he would not have believed them. Not that Harry wasn't keen to get to the top of his profession. It just seemed that sometimes getting there was too far uphill, particularly if he hadn't got as many laughs as he had hoped one night. If the show hadn't gone as well as it should have done, Harry would usually blame himself. Several times the doubts and uncertainties that lurk within every comedian's character would flare up and Harry would wander back to his digs with head bowed low. Depression would be kept at bay with an outlook that saw beyond the immediate hurdle. Always ready as he was to put a brave face on, his closest friends, and in particular Myra, would be the only ones who knew the truth and were able to provide the comfort needed by the saddened clown. You're only as good as your last performance, Harry would repeat to himself.

Fortunately Harry's office seemed to be receiving more calls than ever, and his list of bookings seemed to grow along with Myra's advancing pregnancy. The one-week variety tours continued, and although Harry loved his job, he felt pangs of guilt at leaving Myra at such a time. Torn between the need to earn a living in order to take his imminent responsibilities as a father seriously, and wanting to be with Myra, he felt all he could do was to send a prayer heavenward and leave everything in God's hands.

Harry was soon in Blackpool at Feldman's Theatre, working with equal billing alongside Tony Hancock. As Harry would say, it was in the days before the drink had got the better of Hancock, but the deep insecurities were fairly obvious. Top of the bill was a continental magician named Ali Baba who produced girls from huge empty oil jars. Also on the bill were Levanda, a foot juggler, and a double high-balancing act called The Hintonis. Their act involved the placing of one set of tables upon another until they reached more than fifty feet high. On top of this The Hintonis would balance each other in various unearthly poses which audiences would find quite spectacular. The climax would be when Mr Hintoni balanced the whole weight of his body on the neck of Mrs Hintoni, who was balancing on top of the tables by her fingertips. It always ended in a large round of appreciative applause.

The Hintonis remembered that week well. 'Harry and Tony had both just left the services and knew very little about variety, and so they were in what we called the "wines and spirits" section of the poster. That means their names were the smallest, perhaps even the same size as the printer's!

'The theatre was pretty small too, only seating a few hundred, and was the nearest thing to an old-time music hall that Blackpool had. It was so tiny that there was no room for any dressing rooms backstage, so all the artistes dressed in cubicles arranged under the stage.

'Harry was all right with his marvellous shaving sketch and the Blackpool audiences loved his voice, but they gave Tony Hancock a terrible time. All the pros used to stand in the wings and make predictions on who would make it and who wouldn't. A lot of those who were coming out of the forces hoping to make good, had a type of rawness about them. We all thought Harry was wonderful, though, and could be a big star, but we weren't sure about Tony Hancock. The audience in Blackpool threw pennies on to the stage and booed him off. It was really sad because the theatre manager went down to Tony's dressing room to find him sitting with his head in his hands crying. I think Harry must have gone and reassured him, because somehow he was able to continue, and I know that Harry took him under his wing for a while.'

It was on the first night at Feldman's Theatre that Harry received a telephone call between shows. A hotline from Swansea announced that he had just become a dad. Harry could hardly hold himself still and, straining the telephone receiver to breaking point, he listened as he was told he had a six-and-a-half-pound little girl. They called her Jennifer, and Harry couldn't wait until the weekend when he could travel home to meet her for the first time. Dancing back down to the stage, second house contained the best performance from one bubbling act a Monday night had ever seen in Blackpool.

Between the *Forces Showboat* tours, radio programmes and summer seasons, Harry spent as much time at the Grafton Arms as possible. It would cheer him up on the days he needed it most, and the team were starting to develop their own unique brand of humour that, most of the time, spiralled into uncontrollable laughter. Their meetings were soon being recorded and sent off to the BBC with the view of persuading them to make a series. The BBC's response was to turn the idea down for three years running, with the excuse that the comedy was far too anarchic. Suddenly in 1951 they changed their mind.

Agreeing to a trial recording for a one-off programme entitled *The Junior Crazy Gang*, Michael Bentine, Peter Sellers, Spike Milligan and Harry met Pat Dixon. Pat had the unenviable task of controlling a bunch of lunatics in his beloved studio while producing something on tape that would be cohesive and saleable. He needn't have worried. Although the first recording was certainly akin to a comical firework display, the strength of this new type of humour was obvious, and fitted into the BBC's concern to widen its appeal.

Meanwhile, Harry was increasingly in demand for his stage appearances and had been signed to appear in George and Alfred Black's summer season in Blackpool. Before he began rehearsals came the news from Jimmy Grafton that the BBC had accepted the new show and were offering a series of six programmes to be recorded over several Sundays.

In Gary Morecambe and Martin Sterling's book, *Behind the Sunshine*, they state:

*One of Eric and Ernie's greatest friends to emerge
from these variety days was Harry Secombe. A young
comic himself, he had started to make a big name
in 1951 as a member of the legendary 'Goons' –
Milligan, Secombe, Sellers and, occasionally, Bentine.
Four very funny men who after the war turned stage
and radio comedy on its head for a while, just as
Monty Python would do in the late 1960s for television comedy.*

Secombe had first met Eric and Ernie at the Croydon
Empire. Later, they did pantomime together in Coventry.
Apparently, the man who ran the theatre there had no
sense of humour. Performers tend to look down on accoun-
tants, rather than creators, who run theatres, and he was
one of these. He told the boys that he'd received a letter
complaining about a comedy routine the three of them
were doing together. Eric, Ernie and Harry were quite put
out about this because it was going down well with the
audiences. When Harry was hurt, or attacked in some way,
he would bring out his strongest weapon. His gun was
laughter and the bullets were raspberries.

Between them they concocted a letter saying how good
the show was, and had it sent by Harry's dresser. They
used the address of a friend of the dresser's. The manager
had only had one letter of complaint, and the boy's letter of
praise negated it. He never referred to the matter again.

The variety era was an exciting one, and, apart from the
odd hurdle, Harry considered it a way of life rather than a
job of work. Many of the performers had entertained in the
services, and their humour was of a different kind from
civilian humour. It was what they brought back after the
war. The 'Goon' material, mostly written by Milligan, was
all to lift comedy; and to give it a different kind of feeling.

This 'different kind of feeling' pervaded the studio as much as the broadcasts, as Angela Morley, musical arranger for the new show, remembers. 'In the recording studio there were often quarrels and other contretemps from time to time but Harry was never part of it. He was the stable, beyond-reproach sort of person and nothing unseemly could ever be set at his door. He would be very amusing in the studio, sticking a Spangle in the middle of his forehead or putting his glasses on upside down.'

The Goons quickly became a phenomenon and the four comedians and Jimmy (sometimes known as KOGVOS – Keeper of Goons and Voice of Sanity) celebrated their new recognition appropriately at the Grafton Arms.

Harry had already found Jimmy to be a superb writer and had successfully used several of his songs in his performances. Grafton's obvious ability to understand the business and the performer was eventually to lead Harry to welcome him as his personal manager, a relationship that was to last almost his entire career. Together they agreed that, as Harry's career flourished, they would adopt the attitude of 'the faster you climb, the quicker you'll fall'. Consequently they engineered a slow rise up the show business ladder. So sure were they of their plan that Harry was to turn down an offer by the massively powerful impresario Lew Grade, who was astonished when his suggestion of a season at the London Palladium was not taken up. Although a risky decision at the time, it was a strategy that was to keep Harry at the top of the show business tree for more than fifty years.

Michael Bentine

Co-founder of the Goons, Michael Bentine went on to become one of the country's best-loved comic geniuses. Here Michael explains how his life led up to this historic moment in the early days of his career, and how at first he and his double-act partner seemed to face constant rejection at every audition.

Undaunted, we tried other auditions without getting a single booking. We got plenty of laughs and encouragement from the hardened old pros among the stage staff, but it seemed that our act was too 'different' for safe inclusion in the surprisingly conservative programmes of the post-war music hall.

Our final audition was at the Windmill, the small theatre in the West End, which had become famous as the only nude show in town. Its proud boast, 'We never closed', referred to its unbroken record of performances throughout the London blitz and the rest of the war, including the dreadful V1 buzz bombs and the V2 rocket attacks.

In late 1946, when Sherwood and Forrest did their audition for Vivian Van Damm, the owner, he was about the only West End theatre licensee who gave unknown performers, especially young comedians, the chance to perform in his theatre. To our amazement, among a surprising number of failures at that audition, only two acts got booked. Sherwood and Forrest was one of them. The other was a stocky, ebullient young Welshman with a mop of unruly hair. His name was Harry Secombe.

I sensed an immediate rapport with Harry Secombe. We quickly sized each other up, and liked what we saw.

'What service were you in?' I asked him.

In those first years after the war, it was a question young

men asked each other. Most ex-servicemen felt the bond of shared experience and, in addition, they might have had mutual friends in the forces. In that way I often found out what had happened to friends with whom I had lost contact. Sadly, many of them had been killed or were still missing.

'Army,' the curly-haired comedian replied. 'I was a bombardier in the Royal Artillery. I finished up in Italy and did a bit with CSE (the Army's entertainment unit). That's where I dreamt up my act. How about you, mate?'

'I was RAP. So was my partner. Both of us were aircrew volunteers. I failed my eyesight test, halfway through training, and finished up in Intelligence.'

Harry laughed. It was the first time I was to hear his high-pitched giggle. 'Judging by your act, mate, *no one* is going to believe that. By the way, which side were you on?'

I liked this funny, outgoing Welshman with the ready laugh. Here was someone who had been through the mill and come out the other side still chuckling. Harry Secombe was my kind of bloke. Our long-standing friendship has confirmed that first impression.

Harry was booked into the Windmill a few weeks before Tony and I were due to perform. I went to see his act, which seemed funnier every time I saw it. Performing at the 'Mill' could be quite an ordeal, because often you were faced with the same audience for most, if not all, of the six daily shows. Some stalwarts stayed on from ten o'clock in the morning until the last show, which finished at 10 p.m., moving to seats nearer the stage as others left. They were not there to see the comedians.

Soon, I was writing material for Harry Secombe, who broadcast several times on *Variety Bandbox*, and who was performing in cabaret at various small nightclubs. Together, we dreamed up some original comedy, based on our mutual enjoyment of the movies. In one of the broadcasts our joint effort had clashed with the material the star of the show, Derek Roy, was using. Harry and I got a polite note from Derek's scriptwriter, Jimmy Grafton, pointing this out. He suggested we should discuss the matter in a friendly way over a drink at the Grafton Arms, a pub owned by his family.

In those days, the Grafton Arms was the epitome of public house Victoriana. It only needed sawdust on the floor to make the illusion complete. The landlord, whom I had met once before through a mutual friend, lived over the pub and was anything but a traditional 'Mine Host'. An ex-major of airborne forces, this urbane, clever man was only a few years older than we were. The well-dressed City gent who came downstairs in response to the barman's loud shout of 'Jimmy, two blokes to see yer!' looked more like a Harley Street specialist or a successful banker than a third-generation publican.

He smiled and held out his hand, greeting us with the words, 'You blokes are being too bloody funny. You're upsetting the star of the show. I presume you two gentle-men drink?' We nodded in unison.

'What will it be? Scotch, brandy, gin, or beer?'

'A pint of bitter, please,' we chorused.

Jimmy Grafton's smile broadened. 'A wise choice. At Grafton's we pride ourselves on our ales.'

'Cheers, mate.' Once again we spoke in unison, and downed the fine ale.

Jimmy laughed. It had an honest, fulsome ring to it. 'You two sound like twins. I'm an identical twin myself, so I should know.'

From that evening on, the Grafton Arms in Strutton Ground, Victoria, became our Mecca.

Through Harry I met Spike Milligan.

Interviewers on radio and television often ask me to tell them about the early days of the Goons, expecting a flood of hilarious stories. Oddly enough, the specifics of being a Goon are hard to pin down; the enjoyment, and most of the shared laughter, came from being tuned in to each other rather than from outstandingly funny situations.

The Goon Show came about as the direct result of the evening Harry and I spent with Jimmy Grafton at the Grafton Arms. We took Spike to the pub to meet Jimmy, and later introduced Mine Host to the youthful Peter Sellers.

Yet the show itself did not emerge on BBC Radio until 1951. I would not have missed being with my good friends and *The Goon Show* for a fortune. So long live the Goons and all that we stood for, especially our dedicated attempts to show that 'sacred cows' *all* have hooves of clay.

Norman Vaughan

Sunday Night at the London Palladium, *which he compered for three years, and* The Golden Shot, *are just two of the shows Norman is remembered for. However, he is also known as one of Harry's best mates, and one of the few who know the real Harry.*

If I was doing Harry's *This is Your Life* today, I would say the words 'You look like your grandad without a hat on' behind the screen, and he would know immediately that it was me. This is because when we were in Italy together, I bought this hat called a Borsalino, a famous hat with a very wide brim that the Mafia would wear in all the films. I wore it everywhere thinking I looked very smart, when in fact I must have looked a bloody idiot. We came out of a stage door in Blackpool one day and several girls were standing there waiting. I started to chat one of them up, when she suddenly looked at me and said, 'You look like your grandad without a hat on.' There I was, trying to impress her when she had insulted me. Harry thought it was wonderful and I only have to say these nine words to him today to see him crease up with laughter. When he got the knighthood, I sent him a telegram saying 'You look like your grandad without a hat on.'

It's the stuff Harry does offstage that makes me chuckle most. 'The Scottish Lament' is a Secombe speciality that has never been seen on stage, but always creased me and Harry Worth up in fits. Harry used to do the real events of the day as a poem in a very strong Scottish accent, so strong even a Scotsman wouldn't understand it, except for the last line: 'Och for the nooo, at the vicars' dooo'.

I'm amazed how Harry laughs in the most difficult circumstances. It was just after his stroke that I saw a play which was very good, and I thought Harry would be sensational in the part. So I phoned him up and told him all about it, suggesting he get his agent to look into the possibility of doing it. 'I couldn't lift up my arm to do the drinking bit,' he joked.

My own observation about Harry is illustrated by the story of a lift with half a dozen comedians in it going to the top of a tall building. As it travelled, they would all be making each other laugh. When it stopped at each floor one comedian would get out, until there was only one left with the lift attendant. That comedian would then stand in silence, staring at the ceiling. If it was Harry who was the only one left, he would carry on and make the lift attendant laugh too.

I will remember Harry for making me laugh offstage. Laughter is one of the most important things in the world.

Cyril Fletcher

Cyril Fletcher has been loved and admired through the years as an all-round entertainer, but will be remembered best for his vivid readings of misprints for That's Life *on BBC Television. I'm hoping he won't find any here! When Cyril joined the profession he was twenty-three – he's now eighty-eight – and he was the first manager to use Harry's talents in a show.*

Harry was a front-cloth performer, on stage for perhaps ten minutes, and he was very new at being a variety performer.

He did not in any way let on to the audience that he was new at it. His glorious manic enthusiasm covered all. He rushed on, got on with it, and enjoyed every minute. That was the point of it all – how could an audience not share in Harry's enjoyment? And they did.

It was his shaving act, with lots of laughter from Harry, a dozen raspberries and a desire all the time to get it all over with and get back to the dressing room – but the audience did not want that. They wanted more. He followed with his one-man duet where he sang both soprano and tenor. Hilarious!

He was only twenty-eight years old then, but always he has had the joyous spontaneity of youth, no matter how old he has become.

He is not a complicated man. His whole essence is to enjoy life and for the audience to enjoy it with him. Add to the sense of fun and the sense of humour a glorious operatic voice, and you have a great star. For those of you who can remember Gracie Fields, and her switching from superb singing to sheer lunacy, Harry has the same ability.

Angela Morley

*Born in Leeds, Angela has become one of the most
successful film scorers in the world, and now lives in
Arizona. Her many films include* Watership Down,
The Slipper and the Rose *and* Secrets and Lies, *while
her work with numerous other composers includes*
Superman, Star Wars, Home Alone *and* Schindler's
List. *Despite such an amazing array of film work, she still
remembers her times with Harry.*

I'm proud and feel enriched to have been associated with
Harry throughout the 1950s and 60s. I can tell you that he
is just as kind and warm to everyone around him as people
think he is. He is also even funnier in private than he is on
stage. I made a lot of records with Harry and some of them
were recorded in various European capitals. I remember
being in a nightclub with Harry in Milan at around three
in the morning, crying helplessly, my sides aching with
laughter, praying for him to stop being funny.

There was one occasion in Vienna when, having been
promised an orchestra that would be able to speak English,
I found that none of them could. I hurriedly wrote out a little
German vocabulary of the sort of technical terms I'd need to
use to communicate with the orchestra and correct wrong
notes. I was under a lot of stress having to function in German,
a language that I did not speak beyond 'Can you tell me the
way to the Four Seasons Hotel, please', and I needed the
orchestra's close attention. That's when the musicians found
out that Harry was not just another operatic tenor but much,
much more than that. In fact he was a world-class comic. In
spite of the fact that Harry and I were very good friends, I
profoundly wished he would stop making the orchestra

laugh, because little by little I was completely losing them.

Another time, in the Philips Studio in London, I was conducting the orchestra and also Harry, who I hoped was following me carefully. I was startled to see, out of the corner of my eye, that Harry's singing teacher, Manilo, was conducting him too. I wondered if we were feeding Harry the same information or if Harry had to choose whom to follow!

He is the most generous of men and I will always treasure, among other gifts, a Rolleiflex camera that Harry gave me in 1961. I have the fondest memories of those days and wish Harry and his family all the very best.

Max Geldray

Left behind in England after the war, having escaped occupied Holland, Max was a Dutch soldier with a gift for the harmonica. He was also a highly respected jazz musician and brought much more than just music to the show.

I did quite a lot of recordings for the BBC, which included many pilot recordings, but every one of them came to nothing. So when Pat Dixon, the producer of the Goons, asked me to do one with Harry, Peter, Michael and Spike, I didn't hold my breath. But it seemed like a fun show, and sure enough, several weeks later I received a contract for six shows.

I did the entire series, from the first trial recording until the end. Every time we met we had the best of fun. Harry was such a good man to work with because he was so dependable. Even when I was dragged unexpectedly into the plot and found myself part of the action I knew I was always safe with Harry. In the midst of all that ad-libbing and off-the-wall slapstick, there was no sense of needing to worry what he would do next, I knew I was in capable hands. It always worked out in the end, and, most of all, it would always be funny.

Occasionally during rehearsals they thought it would be a good idea if there was an extra character, and I was immediately hijacked into the sketch. I, along with Ray Ellington and Wallace Greenslade, would also be subject to their gags and throwaway lines, but it was always amiably received. My accent, my age – I was the oldest member of the team – and anything else they could think of was used as a target for fun.

I had been given British nationality in recognition of the part I had played in the war, and this became a butt for many of their in-jokes about me. I think the biggest laugh they had was when they made me say strange words like 'ploogie'! As a result of that, Peter Sellers nicknamed me 'Plooge'. They were wonderful years, and it was a great privilege to be part of them.

Harry is the type of man who is always there when you need him. On one occasion we were doing a Sunday concert together for charity. On such occasions there were so many performers on the bill that it would seem to go on forever and finish in the early morning! Having worked all week in variety, and recorded the Goons on the Sunday afternoon, we were all very tired. I must have seemed a little more stressed than normal or flustered about something, because I shall always remember that Harry came over to me late that night in the theatre and said 'Max, you know, if there is anything you need, I will always be there for you.' For me, that sums Harry up.

Pam Rhodes

Known best for her presentation of Songs of Praise, *Pam is also an author with many titles to her name, including three novels.*

The first time I met Harry was when we were making a *Songs of Praise* programme about 'Love'. We were doing the programme from Majorca, where Harry and Myra have a holiday home. He was such a dear on the telephone because he was concerned that I wouldn't find him when I arrived to interview him, so he offered to wait outside the bank for me. When the crew and I arrived early to make sure we would be on time, there was this little chap standing there at the side of the road waiting for us. It was such a lovely, down-to-earth thing to do, and such a sweet picture that I shall never forget.

He and Myra made us incredibly welcome, and we did an interview all about love and marriage, because they were just coming up to their fiftieth wedding anniversary. When the cameras stopped rolling we just carried on prattling and he wanted to tell me the story of how he and Myra had met. Having just returned from the army, he decided that one Friday he should blow the cobwebs away and go to a dance with some of his friends. At the dance he met this lovely girl; he thought she was smashing and spent the rest of the evening dancing with her. At the end of the evening he asked if she would like to go to the cinema the next night and Myra agreed to meet him on the steps of the Plaza in Swansea High Street.

On the next day when Harry woke up with a hangover, he couldn't remember what she looked like, and wasn't quite sure whether she was worth going to the cinema with. Perhaps she wouldn't look the same in the cold light of day. He hit on the idea of arriving a little early so he could hide behind the pillar at the cinema and check out what she looked like before committing himself. At 5.45 he was happily hiding but by ten minutes to six he considered she was cutting it a little bit fine. By six o'clock she had still not arrived, and by ten past six he decided to give up. Thinking that he had been stood up, he stepped out from behind his pillar just as Myra stepped out from behind hers. The rest, as they say, is fifty years of history.

Danny La Rue

One of Britain's premier entertainers, Danny has recently celebrated fifty years in show-biz, and with seven major West End shows, numerous television and radio appearances, and countless summer seasons and pantomimes behind him, he knows the profession intimately. It was Harry, however, who unintentionally put him on the road to success.

Like Harry, and even when facing many personal tragedies, my faith is the one thing I can still hold on to. It's the strength of this that enables me to carry on working.

The funniest moment in all the television appearances Harry and I have done together was in a Nureyev and Fontaine sketch. I was very slim and Harry was not. I shall never forget seeing him in a tutu, and I told him I could see where he kept his wages!

Harry and I are dear friends, and it seems as if this has always been so. However, when we first worked together on Forces Showboat, it could have been a different story.

Harry couldn't believe his eyes when he first saw me in drag. One night we all went out for a meal when Harry suddenly indicated that he wanted to say something. 'You're a very nice boy, Danny,' Harry said, 'but you're quite unsuited to this show. You haven't really got any proper talent, and if I were you, I'd give up show business and go back to window-dressing!' I took what he said seriously, thought about it for a while, and decided he was right.

Like Harry, I'm a great believer that God guides us in extraordinary ways, because if I hadn't left show business at that point, I wouldn't have gone back to window dressing in Oxford Street. For it was here one day that a producer named Ted Gatty happened to see me as he was passing the window in which I was dressing a mannequin. Ted knew me from the past, was overjoyed and surprised to see me and knocked on the window.

We talked and Ted explained that he had hired the Irving Theatre in Irving Street for a three-week season of revue. He was worried because one of his performers had dropped out at the last moment, and asked me if I would do the job. I said it was very kind of him, but declined. I was very happy in my job, and all the fashion shows that I was involved in, and didn't want to go back into a business that I didn't feel destined for. Ted left disappointed, but came back two weeks later in desperation. He couldn't find anybody, and asked if I would do him a favour and just fill in until he found someone to take over. Otherwise, he explained, he would lose the contract for the show he had with the Irving Theatre.

I agreed with the proviso that my real name wasn't mentioned, in case I lost my job. When I got to the venue it had 'Danny La Rue' on the poster. When I asked who that was, they said it was me! Ted explained how the name had come about: 'Danny La Rue' was chosen from a great singer of the day called Danny Street.

The show went well because they found out that as well as looking good, I could sing and do comedy. From there several producers and club owners saw me and before long I was working nine to five in the shop, seven to eleven at the Irving and one to three a.m. at Churchill's Club. I soon gave up window dressing, but the rest hasn't stopped in fifty years! I have Harry to thank for all that, because if he hadn't persuaded me to leave the business, I would never have been in that shop window when Ted walked past! Thanks Harry!

Later, when we travelled the world together, we arrived in Australia for the Mike Walsh Show, a popular live midday chat show. After we had done our separate performances, Harry and I were interviewed collectively, and Mike asked Harry what advice he had to give to young people going into the profession today. 'Don't ask me,' Harry replied. 'I'm the one who told Danny to give it up!'

When God made Harry Secombe he threw away the mould, he is simply one in a million. I will always remember that sense of deep love in his eyes as he talks to me, and even though the business of show business means we don't often meet up, he never forgets a friendship, and I'm grateful to God for him.

Frank Muir

Scriptwriter, presenter, author and television personality, Frank was adept both behind and in front of the microphone and camera.

Radio comedy matured in the first ten years of peacetime radio, and by the early 1950s the older formats like *ITMA* and Charlie Chester's *Stand Easy*, which depended on techniques inherited from the variety theatre such as quick-fire entrances and exits and rapid little topical jokes enacted in funny voices, were giving way to character comedy, as in the superb *Hancock's Half-Hour*, written by Ray Galton and Alan Simpson; and for many listeners, rising above them all was *The Goon Show* – noisy, irreverent, cunningly smutty, brilliantly inventive and dotty.

The show's original title was *Crazy People*, and Spike Milligan, Michael Bentine and a new writer full of odd ideas named Larry Stephens, who was working as a kind of assistant to Spike, wrote the pilot script. This post did not carry a salary because Spike had no money. He also had nowhere to live. But he met Harry Secombe's half agent, Jimmy Grafton (who shared the other half of Harry with another agent), and Jimmy Grafton owned a family pub in Westminster, the Grafton Arms. He also wrote comedy. Thus the ambitious and gifted little group suddenly had somewhere to meet and write, and Spike had an attic to sleep in.

The producers of *Crazy People* were Pat Dixon and the very young and wildly enthusiastic Dennis Main Wilson. In 1952 their first programme was made. It was not quite right, so back to the drawing board (i.e. pub) they all went, changes were made and the first series of the programme, now produced solely by Dennis Main Wilson, went out on the air with a range of eccentric characters who lasted throughout *The Goon Show*'s long life. These included the cheerful, heroic idiot Neddy Seagoon (played by Harry Secombe), Moriarty the perpetual villain, Colonel Bloodnok, Spike's simpleton character Eccles, whose voice, perhaps unconsciously, echoed Disney's cartoon dog Goofy, and many others.

These inventions, plus bizarre plots and lots of explosions and vigorous sound effects, dismayed, delighted, worried, puzzled and intrigued listeners according to taste. The style came as a breath of stimulating air to broadcast comedy and probably had a greater influence on later generations of writers and performers than any radio comedy programme has ever had.

Jeremy Hoare

Jeremy Hoare is a specialist photographer and was born into a family that enjoyed an appreciation of live theatre. His father, George Hoare, was one of the longest serving managers of London's famous Theatre Royal in Drury Lane.

My father was the last of a breed of managers who worked and lived theatre, and his employment with the famous Stoll Moss Theatre Company for 68 years from 1929 to 1982 is a testament to that.

George had always been interested in theatre history and theatrical traditions and one of his greatest disappointments was that he was not able to become a member of Drury Lane Theatrical Fund. This historic fund is over two hundred years old and was started in 1766 by David Garrick to help members of the permanent company who join it. He really wanted to be part of this tradition, as he was manager at Drury Lane for so long, but unfortunately for George, only members of the cast and stage management are eligible to join.

However, he did make stage appearances throughout the run of *The Four Musketeers*. Harry Secombe was the star of the show and not long into the run had a throat infection which meant that George had to go on stage and tell the audience that Harry could not sing. This was greeted with audible dismay by the audience, but George went on to explain that Harry would still be performing and miming to the songs. This gave Harry the opportunity to get a lot more comedy out of the songs, so George went on every night after that, and it became part of the show.

Leslie Phillips

Veteran comedy actor Leslie Phillips has numerous professional credits to his name from major films and Carry Ons *to television series and his own one-man show. Yet of all those he has worked with, it is Harry who has made a deep impression on him.*

I love Harry Secombe, he is a very special man and the only entertainer I know who remembers everybody's name. A thing I've never been able to do.

He is a delightful person and his family are charming. I don't suppose there can be another person in this crazy world of ours who can be so enchanting.

I could say so much more but its really unnecessary except to say I wish I could be like him.

Syncopating Secombe

It was a way of life, rather than a job.

HARRY SECOMBE

Bernard Shaw once remarked, 'He who tries to analyse humour, proves that he has none.' Somehow, though, Harry had found the key to make everyone laugh, and was very reluctant to lose it by swapping comedy for music, as he was increasingly coming under pressure to do. His voice was so good that several influential producers were suggesting that he consider a career in opera. He had great potential there, they thought. Harry laughed nervously to himself every time someone came backstage and suggested the idea, as it certainly didn't appeal to him. A genuine comic at heart, his singing would always be secondary. Fellow Welsh comedian Wyn Calvin remarked, 'Music was simply a means of making an exit as far as Harry was concerned, nothing more.'

Appearing in that last memorable pantomime at Harry's beloved Swansea Empire, Wyn was aware of how the entertainment business at that time was changing, and how it was this process that eventually caused Harry to change his mind. 'Radio filled theatres, television emptied them,' Wyn explains. 'This was because people wanted to see the favourites they had heard, whereas television had already obliged in this way.

'*Welsh Rarebit* led the way in this respect and was the most listened-to radio programme on the BBC's Light Programme, lasting from the beginning of the Second World War, right through to the late fifties. With a vast audience of between fifteen and twenty million, it was appearing in this revue that brought Harry his fame.'

Mai Jones was the producer of the programme and proved to be quite a character. She had been an accordionist in an all-girl variety act and her experience and understanding of the business soon enabled her to become the country's number one light entertainment producer. Taking over the programme, which originally had a magazine format, she changed it into a variety show at a time when the word 'variety' was still very important. She wanted her show to enjoy a multiplicity of sounds and so welcomed guest singers and comedians alongside its own resident choir.

Music was important, but so was comedy, and Mai began searching for Welsh comedians to fit the bill. There were very few Welsh comedians to choose from at that time; indeed it seemed a contradiction in terms. Wales had a reputation for breeding preachers and singers, not comics. Mai was delighted when she discovered Harry and considered he was a natural for the show. Harry became a pioneer in raising awareness that Wales can be a funny as well as a melodic place.

It is quite ironic, therefore, that although Harry was hired as a comic, it was his voice Mai began to target. He still avoided taking his singing seriously, and much preferred to concentrate his energies on the funny gags, faces and noises, but Mai disagreed. She even persuaded Harry to drop the regular blowing of raspberries that was quite a feature for him. Comedians thrive on the response they get from an audience, and the Secombe raspberry was not only becoming a trademark but provided an onstage insurance policy in the face of a hard audience. Nobody could resist crumpling with hysterics at one of Harry's blasts. Now, Mai was enticing Harry away from the safety of a laugh, and into the development of his voice.

Mai's powers of persuasion must have been quite significant, for Harry has always found it difficult to accept the words of acclamation that have so frequently come his way. 'Tremendous nervousness' was how Wyn described Harry's reaction when confronted with praise for his voice from Mai. 'Comics are generally not good at receiving compliments, often feeling they need to make a gag of it, or even denigrate it. This is because a comic is basically a modest man. Often reticent about the value of his own personality, he gets his laughs by being laughed at, and this denotes the difference between a comic and a comedy actor.'

The desperate fear of walking out on stage and not getting a laugh also keeps a comedian humble. Nerves are an important part of the comedian's toolkit and as Wyn Calvin notes, 'You will never get a tune out of a violin unless its strings are taut. A comic's instrument is his audience, and Harry is an expert at tuning them up. Harry has a unique sense of projecting his humour, a humour that comes from deep inside him. His audiences love him because he loves them.'

Not all comics have the ability to retain this humility, but it is acknowledged that Harry has certainly done so. Having never taken himself too seriously is probably the key here, alongside Myra's down-to-earth love and care of him. 'You may be a star out there,' she is reported to have said one winter's evening as he sat down to relax in his favourite chair. 'But get some coal on that fire, and while you're about it, change that nappy!'

A unique mixture of vulnerability and comic strength has endeared Harry to his audiences. Harry is a sincere person and the persona he projects, whether in film, television, radio or the stage, is that of himself. When facing an audience he does not hide behind a character or guise, he is simply Harry. He is genuine, and his audiences love it.

'To see Harry on the box is only a microcosm of the real man,' explains Wyn. 'When in front of a live audience he projects himself to them, when filming he condenses himself through the camera. The size of his personality is reduced, with the result that he appears very natural. I admire Harry for this because I have been able to make a friend of a microphone throughout my career, but I've never been able to make a friend of a camera. It's quite unique.

'Winston Churchill would never have been the great leader that he was if he had relied on television. While radio made him an inspiring man, his personality would have been too big for television. Somehow Harry has invaded every form of media extraordinarily well. It's his adaptability which is astonishing. He is the perfect practitioner of several different arts.'

It seemed to many that Harry could turn anything into an opportunity for laughter. As Norman Vaughan recalls, 'In 1959, in preparation for entertaining the troops in Cyprus, Harry Worth and I went with Harry to the War Office in London. As we got out of the car, Harry jumped on to the pavement, looked up to where some of the clerks were staring out of the window and shouted up "Hello lads! Where's the war?"

'We all had tea at the RAC Club one afternoon, and I had warned Eric Sykes and Eric Merriman that Harry would make them laugh the whole time. They both looked at me with an "It's not easy to make a scriptwriter laugh, you know" expression on their faces. I told them to wait and see if I was right. As soon as I introduced him to Harry and we sat down, Eric Sykes was, of course, in hysterics.

'There was one line that really got him, as we sat in the very salubrious, starchy surroundings. The waiter came stiffly over to Harry to take Harry's order for tea. "India or China, Sir?" the waiter monotoned. "In a cup with milk," Harry replied.' Eric and Norman were spitting sandwiches and tea everywhere for the rest of the afternoon.

Some of these 'ad-libbed' moments were not intentional, however. On one particular television show he was with Eric Sykes performing the 'Drinking Song', which was eventually used to advertise a branded lager. At the end of the sketch, in which Eric and Harry sat opposite each other in a bar, they banged their glass tankards together and to everyone's surprise the tankards brimming with beer shattered. Harry was literally falling on the floor in un-controllable laughter. He loved those moments when the unthinkable happened, and always seized the opportunity to turn them to the audience's advantage.

Welsh Rarebit was recorded at Swansea's Cory Hall, and Wyn Calvin remembers one night when it was packed after months of applications from people desperate to get seats for their favourite show. 'An old temperance hall, its dressing-room facilities were far from comfortable. The fellas were herded into a tiny vestry at the back of the stage, and the girls managed to get to their basement room via a spiral staircase at the side of the stage. While the girls were able to reach the bathroom, we had no way of relieving the ner-vous tension that every performer feels before going on.

We were simply trapped until it was time to go on stage. However, one of the comedians, who shall remain nameless, was spotted in a corner urinating into a *beer* bottle, in a *temperance* hall!'

Harry's singing became a standard feature on *Welsh Rarebit* and Harry himself began to take more notice of this 'fringe' talent. He started training under Manilo de Veroli, and began to come to the public's attention as a singer.

The development of his voice opened the way for further quality work. Not only could he woo an audience into hilarious submission, he could now serenade them with some of the world's most beautiful songs. Producers were falling over themselves to offer him summer seasons and pantomimes.

Doone Ellerton played the Fairy Godmother opposite Harry's Buttons for three seasons in a row. From 1954 to 1956, the ballet mistress in *Cinderella* enjoyed two consecutive Christmases at the Coventry Hippodrome, followed by one at the Palace Theatre, Manchester. Doone remembers how Harry loved to move away from the script whenever he had the chance of an extra laugh or two. 'During the kitchen scene one night, when I returned disguised as the old woman in the wood,' Doone remembers, 'the puff of smoke and flash went off as normal and there I was transformed into the Fairy Godmother. Harry suddenly shouted out "Oh, look! It's Lorna Goone!" The audience were in hysterics and I remained Lorna Goone for always; I sign letters the same way even now.

'I touched him with the end of my Harry Lauder-type curly magic wand, and switched on the hidden torchlight inside in order to "hypnotize" him so that I could do the coach transformation scene with Cinderella. He was supposed to exit, but there we were throwing lines back and forth at each other, with the audience laughing along all

96

the way. Suddenly out of the corner of my eye I could see the sandbags being lowered on the end of the wires from the flies. These were positioned in preparation for the transformation scene, in which they would be clipped on to the fairy dancers who would then be able to fly around the stage. It was the crew from the Kirbys flying ballet company bringing them in early to encourage Harry to get on with the scene! It wasn't a very subtle way to do it, but I think it worked!

'Harry was such fun to work with, but he always obeyed the instructions of the director – even when one day we were all assembled on stage for notes before opening night and the director's voice from the stalls said, "Harry, would you mind leaving the stage for a moment, I want to have a serious word with the cast!" Harry walked towards the wings blowing raspberries right, left and centre.'

Between seasons, Doone was choreographer with Harry on the famous Coventry Hippodrome Birthday Show in which the Goons appeared live for the very first time. 'They were nervous,' remembers Doone. 'They were used to doing it behind a set of sound screens in a studio, not in front of a live audience. It went very well, though, and the crowds loved them.'

One of Harry's greatest successes in pantomime was as *Humpty Dumpty*. Less frequently produced than many of the other classic pantomimes, it fitted Harry's persona perfectly. The production opened at the London Palladium in 1959, transferring to Manchester the following year, and the reviewers raved: 'This is the pantomime for me,' reported the *Guardian*'s Phillip Hope-Wallace. 'Never have I seen the title role so perfectly cast ...'

'It was well written and superbly produced by impresario Val Parnell, with all the nursery-rhyme characters one could imagine,' remembers Wyn, who took over from

Harry in the title role after Manchester and toured with it for the next six years. 'One of the clever writers was *Dad's Army* creator David Croft, who provided the perfect vehicle for Harry. It all flowed perfectly. When the egg sat on the wall in nursery-rhyme land everything was wonderful, but when the egg fell off the wall, all hell broke loose. The King and Queen of Hearts provided the mucky pastry scene when the Queen made her tarts, and the principal boy was Tommy Tucker, who sang for his supper. Tommy also sang to Mary as he fell in love with her, but when the egg fell off the wall she changed her mind and wanted to marry what had come out of the egg. She was Mary, Mary, quite contrary, of course.'

Also cast in the show was a comedian who was fast becoming one of the best-loved performers on television. When Harry Secombe met Roy Castle, it was the start of a very long and close friendship.

In his autobiography, *Now and Then*, Roy remembers *Humpty Dumpty* vividly:

> *I was to be Simple Simon. The show was peppered with stars such as Alfred Marks, Paddy O'Neill, Gary Miller, Sally Smith, Svetlana, and many more.*
>
> *I turned up imagining the worst. Everyone would have witnessed my pathetic TV series and flop recording. I was cowed and embarrassed.*
>
> *Harry Secombe welcomed me like a long-lost brother and when I started apologizing for myself he steam-rollered over my whingeing by telling me how often he had gone through similar troughs. 'They don't last long, Jim!' he said in his high tenor voice and gave me a mental rubdown with last week's edition of* The Stage. *His generosity and warmth put life back into me and I shall never forget how important*

*that was. He could easily have said 'Tough! That's
show business,' and left me in deeper distress.*

Humpty Dumpty – directed by Robert Nesbitt, the number-
one man for most of the big shows, including the Royal
Commands – proved to be one of the finest and most successful pantomimes the Palladium had ever produced ...
little did I know, but a certain young lady watched that
show who was to play the most important part in the rest
of my life.

The certain lady in the auditorium was named Fiona,
and she was soon to change her surname to Castle. 'The
first time I met Harry was as a chorus girl in his pantomime at Coventry Hippodrome. I'd just left school and
was thrilled to be working with Harry Secombe as top of
the bill with Morecambe and Wise as support.'

Although she didn't realize it at the time, this 1957 show
was to shape Fiona's future, all because of Harry. 'He was
a wonderful top of the bill because he cared about everybody
from top to bottom. As a bottom-of-the-list chorus girl, I was
always amazed when the star of a show said hello to me, but
when Harry greeted me it was as if he really wanted to know.

'There was always a wonderful atmosphere on stage and
off which was conducive to everybody giving of his or her
best, because we were all so full of admiration for him. He
had a gift of being able to encourage each person in the
theatre, which made the whole cast walk round with their
heads held high.'

While Fiona had met Harry, Harry had met Roy. Roy
even called to see Harry while he was appearing in pantomime in Leicester. It's possible that Roy and Fiona
passed in one of the backstage corridors.

Having worked together in pantomime, they next
appeared together in the Royal Variety Show, in which

Harry encouraged Roy to take a second bow. This was unprecedented in a royal show, and reinforced the public's awareness of what Roy could do. 'Harry was standing in the wings watching Roy's performance. When he came off stage at the end of his act, Harry told him that he must take another bow as the audience were calling for him,' smiles Fiona. 'He literally pushed him back on. Harry saw that success, which led to *Castle's In The Air*, a television show for Roy, which wasn't the right vehicle for him and was a disaster. Roy was really depressed and down, but he had already signed up to appear in Harry's new show, *Humpty Dumpty* at the Palladium. He described what Harry did when Roy arrived backstage for *Humpty Dumpty* as like rubbing him down with an oily rag, and then Harry told him to get on with it. This really helped Roy to cope with show business.

'One of the things that Roy always admired about Harry was that there was never any hidden side to him. There was no trumped-up sense of ego, and Harry was a role model for how to cope with success. He showed Roy that it was much harder to cope with success in show business than to cope with failure. One should never let it go to your head, Harry would counsel, always keep your feet on the ground, remembering your roots. The reason that Harry was able to dispense such advice was that he lived it out himself, and found that it worked.'

Conversely, when talking about the art of making people laugh, Harry once confided in Roy, saying, 'Don't ever let them know it's easy!'

Harry and Roy became the best of friends, and it was a strong relationship that was to last and develop greater depth as the years went on. Fiona bumped into Roy on a number of occasions, although it was Eric Morecambe who officially introduced Roy and Fiona to each other, an event which led to Roy's proposal of marriage. St James's Church in Gerrards Cross hosted the wedding, which became one of the show-biz events of the year.

'Harry was the obvious choice to be best man,' Fiona recalls. 'He was the best best man we could possibly have had. Roy introduced him as "a fat lot of good", and Harry got his own back by turning to my parents and saying, "Never mind folks. Don't think of it so much as losing a daughter, as gaining a weekend gardener."' The whole reception was falling around the floor, intoxicated not by wine, but by the very best of British humour.

Two years later Fiona gave birth to their first baby, Daniel. Roy was still working alongside his old mate, and felt that such a family occasion couldn't be better celebrated than with the Secombes. 'Roy had signed up to be Sam Weller in the first tour of *Pickwick* prior to going to Broadway,' says Fiona. 'Daniel was only seven days old when we had him christened at St Dunstan's Church in Cheam, near where Harry and Myra lived. Their oldest daughter, Jennifer, was Daniel's godmother. The next day both families left together for the tour. It was amazing timing!'

What was even more amazing was the care that Myra showed Fiona while they were in the USA. Daniel was Fiona's first baby, and it wasn't easy travelling so far in a foreign country with a week-old baby. 'I was so insecure I thought I'd never keep the baby alive,' shudders Fiona. 'I felt so lost, but Myra was just brilliant. She was like a travelling nurse, advisor and supporter all rolled into one.'

Roy had already been a godfather to Harry and Myra's son, David. Jennifer, their eldest, had arrived during that Blackpool season of 1949; Andrew came along next, then Katy and finally David. Each birth in the Secombe family was a celebration that Harry would host with glee. He was as involved with his children's lives as he was involved with Roy and Fiona's. Whether it was making sure he kept his diary clear so that he could take Katy to her first day at school, or inviting Andrew and Jennifer to help him collect his CBE, Harry was always at the heart of family life.

Harry loves to be the clown, and nothing makes him happier than when he can hear the sound of the guffaws he has himself generated, as Fiona explains. 'Eric Morecambe was similar to Harry in that you couldn't have a serious conversation with him for more than half a minute, it doesn't matter if it was the Queen or whoever. But neither did the laughter stop him from being sincere. As observers of human beings, comedians are brilliant at seeing through any hypocrisy to the reality of life. I think Harry is a master of this.

'Harry naturally sees the funny side of things which others can't. I've got myself in serious trouble a few times trying to emulate him, and making a complete mess of things. In trying to make one silly comment to a woman one day she took me seriously, and didn't talk to me for over a year! I've learnt that Harry is unique and now I leave the quips up to professionals like him!

'Like Roy and Eric, Harry is not a gag teller, and whenever we had dinner together they had the ability to sit at a table and make everyone crease up within seconds through caricaturing real life. The three comedians bounced off each other wonderfully, but as wives we didn't feel left out, we'd just sit and laugh. Events like this were such a support to all of us living in the strange and isolating world of show-biz.'

Why has Harry never been tempted to 'stray' in a profession renowned for its relaxed attitude to relationships? The answer lies in Myra, suggests Fiona. 'Ever since they met they have recognized the value in each other. As one

Hollywood star has since commented, "If you've got steak at home, why go out for a hamburger?" Harry and Myra have made sure it has been steak all the way for each other, and have given a hundred per cent of their time, attention and care to their marriage because they considered it so important.'

Being needed is also an important part of a marriage, says Fiona. 'I loved Roy more when he was a failure, because he needed me. When things don't go right and the world doesn't want you, when the show is a failure and the critics have slated you, who have you got to come home to? I believe that part of their successful marriage is due to the fact that Harry had Myra to come home to. She was there to need him, and tell him he was wonderful and to love him just when he needed that reassurance. It's like the song from the show *The King and I* ... "He may not always be what you want him to be, but now and then he'll be something wonderful."'

Harry and Myra were obviously suited to each other from the start, and grew up in an era when divorce was not an easy option. Instead of walking away from their problems, they worked through them. While Myra provided a happy and comfortable home, Harry provided security and love and made Myra feel special. In their own way they are a romantic couple, perhaps most of all in the way they show respect for one another. Harry would make sure Myra got the best seat in the house at a first night and would make her queen of the after-show party. Although Myra was happy to dress up for important events, she was equally as happy at home, and always found it hard to leave the children behind.

The father figure of kindness personified by Harry was not just reserved for the family. He would be as happy helping out the stranger at the stage door struggling in great personal difficulties as he would his brother. Sometimes this would mean he was open to being taken advantage of by strangers, but he never complained, nor stopped looking for ways in which he could support and encourage.

Harry's hand was offered to anyone he came into contact with. He wanted to look after the people he felt responsible for, and they felt they were part of his family. Certainly anybody signed up to do a Harry Secombe show knew for a fact that they were in for a treat. Not only were the shows superbly produced under Harry's discreet but watchful eye, but Harry was always a very happy and generous person to work with. When living and working together so closely, having a happy leading man makes an enormous difference to everyone in a company, from the wardrobe department to orchestra and chorus girl. Harry would engender even more of a sense of team with his backstage parties, known as 'Harry's Happy Parties'.

On longer runs, Harry's Happy Parties would be held on a regular, monthly basis. Between shows, at a time before videos, Harry would pass round a catalogue of 16mm films that were available to hire. The company decided between them what film they would watch later that week. Hiring the latest cinema releases, Harry invited each member of the show from lowly dresser to theatre manager to enjoy them. Wine, cold chicken and rolls were provided and kept everybody as one on a show in which the set would often prevent everybody meeting each other.

If there is any kind of trouble on a show, cliques on both sides of the argument form very quickly. Harry's solution was to commandeer two vacant dressing rooms and make them into a green room where the company could get together over tea and coffee between shows. If there were any grievances, they could be talked about and aired here.

It all made for a cheerful company and Harry's shows became famous as some of the happiest to work on.

This sense of comradeship even extended to the pressurized atmosphere of the film studio. After his roles in *Svengali*, *Jet Storm*, *Davy* and *Penny Points to Paradise*, Harry was delighted to be the first signed up for the new feature film of *Oliver!* The 1968 film of the musical became a great success and after Harry's experience in *Pickwick*, which had opened three years previously, he was ideally cast as Mr Bumble.

As David Roper reports in his biography of the show's composer, Lionel Bart, the film was an instant success:

> When the film was released after its Royal Premiere in the presence of Princess Margaret at the end of September 1968, Barry Norman and Alexander Walker were among those who accorded it unanimous praise and endless superlatives. Walker's review begins: 'Oliver! is a musical that couldn't give you a spoonful more if you got down on your knees and begged for it. It gives all it has got, and a tremendous amount of enjoyment that turns out to be. It represents the canonization of Mr Moody in theatrical history, the restoration of Sir Carol Reed to the top flight of film directors and the consummation of Lionel Bart – for unless they do Oliver! on ice (and knowing Mr Bart they very well may), what more can human ingenuity do to it?'

The last word goes to Ian Christie, writing in the *Sunday Express*: 'The film cost £4 million to make, and as far as I am concerned every penny was well spent. As far as musicals go this is exactly my bowl of gruel, a feast at which even Oliver himself couldn't ask for more.'

By the close of 1969 *Oliver!* was acknowledged as the most successful British film ever made. It had cost between £3 and £4 million to make and in those first twelve months had enjoyed box-office returns of £20 million, and that amount came from only twenty-six cinemas out of 1,700 in Britain, and a couple of hundred out of several thousand in America. And its appeal was strikingly universal: in a rare achievement for a British film, it was decided in Moscow that *Oliver!* was suitable for Soviet audiences.

Its success was due in no small way to the close-knit and clever casting. Again, members of the cast were thrilled to be working with Harry, who proved himself to be such a professional when in front of the cameras, but so down to earth when he was behind them. Jack Wild, who played the Artful Dodger, recalls: 'Funnily enough I never saw Harry when we were shooting *Oliver!* as all our scenes were separate. When I was there filming one day, Harry wasn't. A lot of people talked about what a nice man he was. I did, though, do his TV show with Ron Moody. I can't remember what we actually did, but I do remember him vividly. He was and still is an absolute diamond geezer! Not only is he very funny and entertaining, but also more importantly, always showing genuine love for his fellow human being. He seemed forever on hand in the studio to help anyone who needed it. Very rare these days, but that's our Harry. Always the same. That's what happens when you keep a close family together like he does.'

Harry also has a unique ability to show compassion without offending people with an overt display of charity. 'I remember Harry being very kind to me, but not overbearingly so, when we were appearing on a bill together in Cardiff,' remembers Wyn Calvin. 'I had to come to the show that night straight from my father's funeral, and he popped into my dressing room before the show and smiled his concern for me. He was always very supportive.'

This genuine 'niceness' prevented the most insecure performers in the business from becoming jealous of him. After all, here was a man who had made his way from the back of an army truck to the London Palladium within ten years; had starred in so many revues and pantomimes it was hard to remember them all; and had helped create a radio series that would probably last for ever. Any sort of unpleasantness towards Harry would be, as one show-biz friend described it, 'spitting on the altar'.

Fiona Castle

At speaking engagements worldwide, Fiona recounts her experiences of life in show business with her late husband Roy, and the frailty of life alongside the necessity of faith. She and Roy have been friends of the Secombe family for many years.

Harry is the most generous man I've ever met, and will give freely when he sees a need. You could never out-give Harry because he always gives back double. It's a very biblical principle. He has always known it's right to give, and if people decide to abuse that, it isn't anything to do with him. Most people in this business think of Harry as a giver.

June Whitfield

One of our best-loved actresses, June has been helping us to laugh for many years.

Sir Harry is justifiably regarded as a brilliant entertainer. He is also a charmer, a very nice man and a national treasure. I am an ardent fan.

Russ Conway

A highly talented musician, with several number one hits to his credit, Russ was one of the first piano entertainers to reach the top of the charts, and shared the Palladium stage with Harry.

What can I say about Sir Harry Secombe that has not been said by hundreds, even thousands of others who have had the great joy of knowing and working with him?

Perhaps I have a slight edge in that he kindly recorded one of the songs I wrote with Norman Newell back in the early sixties. This was called 'The Song of the Valley' and I still play it often. He made such a beautiful and touching recording of the song that no one else could repeat it and I shall forever be grateful to him for that.

Working with him in many fields was enlightening, joyful and always full of fun. Performing along with Jimmy Tarbuck, Anita Harris and many others at the London Palladium in *London Laughs* in 1966 was pure contentment for me, especially being part of a Harry Secombe bill.

In fact there was a lovely old donkey named Bill in the show, and nightly we would wait to see what little trick Bill had up his sleeve or down his leg. None of us should have been doing it as we all had strict orders never to feed the donkey, particularly between performances. Harry and Jimmy, however, would secretly nip down to the area that the donkey was kept in and offer him a few extra tempting morsels.

It was during the second half of the show that the donkey made his grand appearance, pulling the cart containing Thora Hird and Freddie Frinton in the opening 'Pearly Kings and Queens' scene. As the band struck up 'My ol' man said follow the band', we would all watch expectantly to see if the ass would actually perform from his rear end, egged on by Harry and Jimmy. It was all done in the best possible taste, but when the donkey actually relieved himself for the first time, we were all so creased up we could hardly sing the words. At that moment, the audience must have wondered why the entire company on stage were gazing up to the ceiling. Thereafter we were constantly caught between the hope that it would happen again, and the fear of firm retribution from the company manager.

Working with Harry, I have found him equipped with a sense of humour unmatched by anyone else I have ever met in the business. He is loved by all those who know him and by millions who may never have met him, but have experienced his mighty generosity with his comedy, which is sometimes at the expense of his own well-being. He's always stood tall, albeit in a short way, in the eye of his admirers.

Harry is a very good human being who deserves every single accolade ever bestowed upon him. Live long, Sir Harry, and be happy and content.

Nick Page

*A well-known radio voice familiar to listeners to Radios 2
and 4, Nick has interviewed many from the world of the
media, arts and entertainment industries, including
Sir Harry.*

I think the great strength of Harry is 'WYSIWYG' – what
you see is what you get. The great integrity that meant that
when the red light went on he didn't have to change into a
public persona, as some performers do. The Harry I interviewed was the same thoughtful, fun, gracious, bubbling
personality who came over on air. Image and substance
were integrated. A rare delight.

Graham Stark

*Director, actor and close friend of Peter Sellers, Graham
says that working with Harry was like a dream come true.*

If it was fun directing Peter in *Simon, Simon*, it was a joy to
direct Harry Secombe in the picture *The Seven Deadly Sins*.
    He was a professional's professional: the first on the set
in the morning, absolutely word perfect, he would accept
any kind of directing without a murmur. I watched Harry
with fascination, for he was such an extraordinary contrast
to Pete. They'd worked together for so many years in the
Goons, were close friends, shared exactly the same sense of
humour, were both talented performers, and yet in Harry
was a contentment, and a joy in living, that Peter never
seemed able to achieve. The answer of course was Myra.

Ship Ahoy! – on holiday with Myra, Andrew and Val and Lynn Doonican.
Associated Newspapers

Wrong show, wrong sketch? No, just Harry singing a *Rose Marie* duet with Eartha Kitt for *Secombe and Friends*. *Personal Collection*

Chief comic and best man at the wedding of Roy Castle and Fiona Dickson in 1963. *Hulton Getty*

A bevy of beauties and one Goon – Harry surrounded by the Pamela Davis dancers during a rehearsal for the Royal Variety Performance of 1969. *Hulton Getty*

Harry must be a professional giver, but this time it's his blood that is wanted, at the army supply depot in Aldershot. *Hulton Getty*

Variety club pals pay tribute to Harry at a special luncheon given in his honour in 1971. Back from left to right: Eric Sykes, Jimmy Edwards, Jimmy Tarbuck, David Coleman, Michael Bentine. Front from left to right: Hylda Baker, Donald Houston, Davy Kaye, Bruce Forsyth. *Hulton Getty*

On the eve of his 50th birthday Harry tries daughter Katy's school hat on for size. *Hulton Getty*

Bi-focals? With pal Eric Morecambe. *Rex Features*

Two Harrys and a Vera – Sir Cliff Richard, Dame Vera Lynn and Harry at a variety club luncheon. *Hulton Getty*

Grandparents and grandchildren. Emily and Sam relax at the Secombes' Majorcan retreat. *Camera Press*

I've got a lovely bunch of.............? Spike and Harry. *Hulton Getty*

Which one smells the worst? Kiri Te Kanawa and Harry in a favourite sketch. *Camera Press*

Once a knight is enough! Receiving his knighthood at Buckingham Palace in 1981. *Hulton Getty*

'I don't believe it!' Mister Pickwick himself. *Camera Press*

With old friend Roy Castle as Sam Weller, on the final tour of *Pickwick*.
Photograph by John Timbers

'I did it Highway!' *Rex Features*   Harry and Myra, 1999. *Rex Features*

Gillian Lynne CBE

*With many years of experience in the business, and great
successes with such shows as* Phantom of the Opera *and*
Cats, *Gillian is renowned as one of the finest
choreographers of our time.*

I starred in a pantomime called *Puss in Boots*. I was Puss.
The broker's men were played by Eric Morecambe and
Ernie Wise, the young love interest for the girls was played
by Terry Kendall (father of Kay) and the great actor and
comedian Harry Secombe played the leading broker's man.

I was very conscious of playing the lead role and probably a little pompous. Of course Eric and Ernie and Harry
constantly improvised. One night I went to Harry and said,
'Dear Harry, I have not had the correct cue lines for the last
four nights and is it possible we could return to the script?'
Whereupon he did return to the script and all the laughs
went!

I went back rather rapidly to say to them all, 'Say whatever you want, and I'll find a response I can reply to!'

Val Doonican

*A leading singing star and entertainer for over thirty years,
with gold discs and numerous television series to his credit,
it is Val's charming and relaxed style on stage that still
endears him to listeners and viewers alike.*

Both my wife and I have known Harry as a friend over
many years. Lynn was part of a very long season he did at
the London Palladium back in the late fifties. The show

was *Large as Life*, and also included Terry-Thomas, Eric Sykes, Harry Worth and Hattie Jacques. Needless to say, he appeared as guest on my TV show many times over its twenty-four years run. Goodness me!

To me, Harry represents all the very best qualities of our profession. The talents, the personality, the professionalism, that sheer reliability. Above all, he's a very nice gentleman.

Doone Ellerton

Famously renamed after a Christmas season of
Cinderella *with Harry, Doone pays tribute to the*
Harry she knew offstage.

Harry is a wonderful man who is tremendous fun to work with, and in fact makes it unlike work at all! Where he was so very clever was in throwing a company party, not after the first night, but after the final dress rehearsal. The result was that all the company relaxed, and the first night went like a bomb.

John Short

Having come from a show business family that has spanned several generations, John himself has spent a lifetime in the live theatre. Working as company manager for many of the top names in entertainment, he is now resident manager at the Churchill Theatre in Bromley, and is responsible for the finely tuned day-to-day running of this popular venue.

As a boy, it seemed that every time I saw Harry he was doing something different. Pulling those amazingly silly faces, playing a strange musical instrument, or singing a magnificent aria while everything around him fell apart. He seemed to be able to turn his hand to anything. This is the true hallmark of a good all-round entertainer.

One of my most treasured possessions is a photograph of Harry with my father, who was a popular Scottish singer called Buddy Logan. As part of the famous Logan family, he had spent a lifetime touring the variety halls of his day. Having arrived in Blackpool, Buddy performed the usual professional courtesy of popping in to greet fellow acts also appearing in the town. At the Opera House was dear Harry, second on the bill to the singer Allan Jones, father of Jack Jones.

Harry greeted my father and having invited him to his tiny dressing room, made the stranger feel quite at home. They were soon into all the banter of how terrible the land-ladies' digs were, and how the audiences in each town were treating them. Suddenly in walked Eve Boswell, another famous crooner of the day. She offered to take a photograph of my father with Harry. Somehow she managed to include her starry-eyed pet dog in the picture too, and Harry just beamed in his usual way.

Many years later, I was invited to watch Harry rehearse *The Plumber's Progress*, a new comedy play written especially for him. Sitting in the illustrious surroundings of London's Prince of Wales Theatre I watched in silence as the scene unfolded. Sometimes directors are known to suffer from temper tantrums, but this guy was somehow obsessed with the way in which the door should be opened. Should it be slowly, or quickly? Should it be from the left or the right? Perhaps with a great amount of flurry, or quietly and unobtrusively? I wanted to shout out 'Just open the door!' Harry, with all the patience of a saint, tried every suggestion that the director made without one word of complaint. It was obvious that Harry was a master of comic timing, yet his humility allowed him to listen and learn from others. What a true professional.

Max Bygraves

Max first worked with Harry on two of the most popular BBC radio series, Educating Archie *and* They're Out. *Benny Hill, Jimmy Edwards, Harry Secombe and Spike Milligan had also passed the audition and with this package Max says the studio was a riot. An amazing audience of thirty million listened to these series.*

Harry is a wonderful guy and a good friend.

Dame Joan Sutherland

Joan's voice remains one of the marvels of our century.

The opening night of *The Mastersingers* was on 28 January in a production designed by Georges Wakhevitch. The settings and costumes were very traditional medieval and the cast predominantly English-speaking, working well together. I enjoyed my scene with Sachs (James Pease) and the Quintet very much; however, the critics didn't seem to think the whole thing had quite jelled, but it would probably settle down in due course. Geraint Evans singing his first Beckmesser was very well received. There were five performances all told until the end of February.

On Sunday 17 February, the whole cast assembled on stage at 9.30 a.m. in costume and make-up to film the final scene of the opera. This was for an English movie (*Davy*) starring Harry Secombe as a would-be opera singer with Adele Leigh playing the part of his girlfriend. I think we were there all day and Harry Secombe was keeping us amused, being more like his *Goon Show* characters than Walther von Stoizing. Yes, in the film he made it to Covent Garden!

Wyn Calvin

Born in West Wales, Wyn has lived in his family home since the age of eleven, when his father bought it for a thousand pounds in an air-raid shelter during a bomb attack on Cardiff! A seasoned variety performer, Wyn is known as 'The Prince of Welsh Laughter', and is blessed with a very rich baritone singing voice, which he uses to good effect in his role as a highly regarded pantomime dame. Hugely involved in after-dinner speaking all over the world, Wyn is a member of the Grand Order of Water Rats.

From one Welsh comic to another I pay tribute to Harry, especially for his warmth both on and off stage. He has a tremendous amount to give both as a performer and a friend. I'm proud of him too, because he has been the classic example that the Welsh have a good sense of humour as well as a good sense of music. Professionally, and in a business that has resorted to more and more adult material, Harry has retained standards when all around seem to be losing theirs.

Sailor Secombe

I owe it all to Myra. If it was a lottery, I got a winning ticket!!

HARRY SECOMBE

'If you get Harry talking about his wife, children and grandchildren he simply bubbles over with pride. He is not only a proud father, but a proud grandfather too, a real family man,' says Fiona Castle. 'I saw him with his granddaughter the other day and he was so sweet playing with her and sitting her on his lap. It's not been an easy time for all their children as they have grown up, but Harry was always there to offer the hand of support, whether it was a marriage crisis or a traumatic career ride. Despite being away a lot, he's never been the absent father.'

Although the difficulties of being a show-biz dad to four small children were sometimes to cause family arguments, Harry did his best to make sure it was as natural a family life as he could make it. Although juggling show business and family was not easy, somehow Harry and Myra have managed it with great success, and there are no skeletons in the Secombe cupboard – a fact that is hard for the press moguls to believe sometimes.

The Secombe residence was famously situated at 129 Cheam Road, Sutton for thirty-two years. Its site on a main road typified their determination to be part of a community rather than remain aloof. The Secombes endured many a knock on the door from strange-looking characters asking for charity, and none would ever be sent away empty-handed. As one friend remarked, 'Harry and Myra are both completely classless. No matter who it is, they will neither turn their heads away nor be over-engrossed. With all the fame and glory that Harry has known, he must have an enormous inner strength and character not to have let it change him for the worse.'

Drivers would pass their door on their way to a hard day's work, glance across at the large detached house, and recall something that they had seen Harry do on television recently. It brought a smile back to their faces and made life bearable again.

The cricket ground opposite the house offered a wonderful opportunity for Harry to form the all-star Secombe team, who would eagerly, if not skilfully, play against a local eleven. The Christian Science Church just along the road was converted into a four-hundred-seater venue named after him. The Secombe Theatre now boasts a whole array of shows: touring productions, children's shows and pantomime. Harry opened the venue and is proud to be associated with it.

Supporting local theatres has been one of Harry's ongoing concerns, and he went one year to see the dress rehearsal of Fred's local Gilbert and Sullivan Society's production of *The Gondoliers*. He was most impressed, even offering the soprano and tenor a job on one of his next shows. Family and work commitments prevented them from taking up the proposal, but they were suitably flattered!

Sadly this was at a time when their mother was very ill, having been diagnosed with bowel cancer. 'I'm very sorry,' explained the surgeon to Harry and Fred, 'but we were unable to remove all the cancerous growth. She will enjoy reasonable health for about five years, but at the end of five years it will recur and you must be prepared for her to pass away.'

The boys decided not to tell Father. 'We kept it from him because he would have gone to pieces,' remembered Fred. It was just as the doctor had said. Harry had by this time bought a flat for their parents and visiting one day, Mother said to Fred, 'Don't ever be afraid to die. I saw your grandmother this morning, here as plain as a pikestaff, at the foot of my bed. Never be afraid to die,' she repeated. A few weeks later and she was gone.

It pulled the family together once more, as Carol came down from Lincoln to look after Father and the family as they grieved.

The celebrity status now afforded to Harry meant the story was splashed all over the press, but his stature in the business usually made the family very proud. It was Fred who found some aspects a little irritating. 'So often I would be in the middle of visiting someone when they would say "How's Harry then?" Some seemed to want to get to know me because of who I knew. Instead of Fred I was Harry's brother. It was very frustrating when this happened, particularly when my fellow clergymen asked me to see if I could get Harry to come down and open their garden fetes and things. Harry always understood the pressure on me, and that's what made it bearable.'

The occasional interruption while enjoying a family meal in a restaurant was accepted as par for the course, but the constant demand for Harry to perform in some way with an autograph, funny voice or raspberry was often tedious. Harry never showed his frustration. Always aware that the public were the ones that hired him, he treated every fan, from obsessive nutcases to ardent admirers, with courtesy and grace.

Holidays were the means of escape, and often as far away as possible. Not that the Secombe family wanted to leave everybody behind. Often they joined in with other people's holidays, as fellow performer Val Doonican fondly remembers.

'In common with many of my fellow workaholics, I've never been all that enamoured with the prospect of going away on holiday. I've loved it from the family's point of view, of course, and look back on our many trips, when the children were younger, with great affection. Now, as I get a little older and the pressure of work has greatly decreased, I find that my attitude towards going away for a break is fast approaching what it should have been all along. Up to the time when Lynn and I got married, in fact, I'd never really bothered to go on holiday at all. I suppose I thought my work was like a never-ending vacation.

'It has been suggested to me on occasions, that perhaps I never found the right kind of holiday for me personally. Who knows, maybe my ideal is waiting somewhere out there and we simply haven't got together. I should clarify the situation by saying that I love just staying at home, using the time to catch up on my hobbies. In recent times we've acquired a little holiday home abroad, and I intend using its peace and quiet to make up for lost time. I want to read all those good books that I never got round to because of my busy life.

'My initiation into the more exotic kind of holidays came about in the mid-sixties through some friends of ours. The husband had achieved quite exceptional success with the company for which he worked, and was invited by them to spend some time in the West Indies as their manager there. Before leaving, the family kindly invited Lynn and me to come out and spend a holiday there as their guests, whenever we felt like it. Since we were busy settling into our new home at the time, we felt the idea to be a bit out of reach financially. Fortunately my career was coming along in leaps and bounds, and pretty soon we began viewing the idea as a real possibility.

'The following winter found us both enjoying the warm sunshine of Jamaica, not to mention the warmth of hospitality extended to us by Terry and his wife Bobbie, and their young family. After that initial introduction we made regular visits with our girls to both Jamaica and Barbados, sharing the joys of the Caribbean with fellow members of the entertainment world, like Harry and Myra Secombe, David and Barbara Coleman and their respective families.

'One sunny morning Harry, David and I went on a deep-sea fishing trip. An elegant cabin cruiser with a crew consisting of two young lads came and picked us up from the beach adjoining our hotel.

'"Well, Val, old son," I thought, climbing over the side, "this is a hell of a long way from the piece of string, bent pin and tin of worms. This is the real stuff."

'The young skipper, inviting us to make ourselves comfortable, began pouring three very generous beakers of rum punch. Dressed in floppy sun hats, swimming shorts and little else, we settled down, sipping our local brew and wishing the folks at home could see us. Meanwhile our three fishing lines, baited and cast over the stern, were being made secure in the special housings which allowed them simply to get on with the job, as we headed seaward.

'Each line has a little of its slack taken up before cast-off. This is held securely by a kind of clothes-peg device. At the first signs of tension on the line the slack is suddenly released, accompanied by a warning "crack" as the peg snaps shut, signifying a bite. That's usually the signal for novices such as myself to leap out of their seats, running madly about the place wondering what to do next. Then follows a most fascinating piece of theatre, in my opinion. The young expert, with great enthusiasm, grabs the line and, having invited you to jump into the work-seat to which your personal rod is attached, he slowly and skilfully brings your fish home.

'All the time you're acting as a kind of willing helper, and sharing in the excitement. The job completed, he pats you on the back and shouts, "Well done, sah, you got 'im and he's a beauty, too."

'It's a wonderful morale-booster, especially later as you stroll up the beach, a large kingfish slung over your shoulder. I knew that Harry had done it all many times before, so deep down I said a little prayer that the fish would pick him first, then I could sit and watch.

'Goodness knows how many rum punches later Harry held the floor, or the deck, with endless stories of his days in the forces and his years with the Goons. Suddenly, we heard the warning click and one of the lines took up its slack. It was Harry's. He leaped into action, assisted by one of our young experts.

'"Take it easy now, sah," he said in his lovely West Indian accent. "Don't rush 'im, sah."

'A huge kingfish leaped from the water, some distance from the boat, only to disappear again into the depths, while David and I watched, and shouted our encouragement. Well, whether it was a case of Harry doing all the right things, or the fish's being a bit of an amateur, I don't know, but in no time, we were pulling the gleaming catch on board. He was a beauty indeed, and I must say I felt a bit sorry for him as he thrashed about there on the floor in the stern of the boat.

'Harry must have felt that sense of guilt also, because no sooner had the kingfish shown signs of ending his struggle, than Harry took him by the fin and started apologizing profusely.

'"I'm sorry, my old lad," he told him, "it could have been any of them out there; you were just passing at the time. Nothing personal, you understand."

'The fish showed no sign whatever of accepting any excuses, but just lay there motionless. Then came Harry's final tribute to his victim. Holding the blue-coloured tail between his palms and gazing out to sea, he burst into song in that rich tenor voice:

'"Your tiny hand is frozen, let me warm it into life."

'His familiar tones echoed across the beautiful blue carpet of water with just the odd fish popping its head up to see what the hell was going on. David and I were busy laughing with Harry, never thinking for a moment that this was anything unusual for Mr Seagoon. Our laughter turned to hysterics, however, as we turned around and caught sight of our young captain and mate, and the look of total bewilderment on their faces. You can well imagine, two youngsters who didn't know Harry from Adam, standing there thinking he must have lost his mind.

'"Who is that maan?" one of them asked, smiling. We smiled back, reassuring them that he was quite sane and did this sort of thing for a living. One of them turned to Harry and said, "What's your name, sah?"

'"Secombe," shouted Harry.

'"Where you come from, sah?" the lad asked. I knew what was coming next and couldn't wait to see the lad's face.

'"I come from Wales," Harry told him.

'"Where, sah?" the boy said, looking puzzled; he'd obviously never heard of Wales.

123

'"Wales," Harry repeated, "Wales, boy." Then, slapping his huge torso with the palms of his hands, he said, "With a figure like mine, I couldn't very well have come from Sardines, could I?" This was followed by the typical Secombe laugh and a raspberry. The young boy looked at all of us with a blank expression. They couldn't be expected to see the joke really. They'd probably never heard of a place called Sardines, either.

'It's a very interesting study, trying to analyse how well certain types of humour will travel. Like wines, some will be acceptable on arrival, while others will just die in transit. Being Irish, and having been weaned on my own native humour, I've lived through countless examples of one man's humour being another man's blank look. Phrases or sayings which were so much part of my early life can, when casually introduced into a conversation, bring a snigger of approval from some, or nothing more than a puzzled look from others ... It's an enviable talent, making people laugh, night after night, year in year out.'

Holidays for Harry were a vital part of switching off from the never-ending calls for appearances, interviews, new series and shows. Not that Harry ever took it all for granted. He thanked God for it every day. Any offer of work passed through his agent's office was always treated with the utmost respect and consideration. Harry saw his life in show business as a privilege and therefore treated it as such.

Celebrity status can be very wearing whether on holiday or not, but Harry has never allowed it to appear to be so. On visiting his agent, he would often insist that he reply to his fans personally, a task that would sometimes take him many hours, but one that he continues to the present day. He still receives hundreds of letters, many inspired by his role in the Goons. Some of these are sent from around the

world and particularly from across the water, where Dick
Baker runs America's Goon Show Preservation Society.

Dick and Harry developed a pen-pal relationship in
which Harry was always keen to reply, and was finally
rewarded for his kindness. Harry would send his personal
reply within a few weeks of receiving each letter.

September 20, 1985

Harry Secombe
St. James Place
London
England

Dear Sir Harry:
*I bring you greetings from your many admirers in the
colonies! I became a fan of the Goon Show about a
dozen years ago when an Australian friend living in
this area, Hal Farmer, perceived that I might enjoy
Goon humor and gave me several shows on tape. His
assessment was right; I quickly became a bit of a
fanatic, corresponding with people all over the world
to acquire as many shows as I could.*

*I became the semi-official USA Goon Show
Archivist in 1976 ... I have enclosed my list of shows
and other broadcasts of interest to Goon fans; if there's
anything I should have and don't, please let me know.*

*About the enclosed photograph of me with my auto-
mobile: some years ago, the state of Virginia began
offering what we call 'vanity' license plates; one pays
an extra fee and selects one's own license number –
within reason. The limitation is six characters plus an
optional hyphen, so 'BLOODNOK' (my favorite
character) and 'SEAGOON' were out; I selected*

'C-GOON' as the best hope of announcing my Goon Show affiliation to all. Unfortunately, I have to report that after three years of driving around with such license plates, not a single soul has recognized the plates for what they mean.

Once I was committed to carrying the Neddie Seagoon/Harry Secombe banner wherever I travelled, I began stuffing myself with food and drink in order to bring my corporeal representation into line with my automotive announcement. Just when I thought that I had succeeded (as shown in the photo), I received the attached newspaper clipping from a Goon in Bermuda, which informed me that the former fat, short and dreadful Neddie had callously shed four stone, throwing a sneaky curve (to use American baseball slang) to those of his fans who had so assiduously emulated his lifestyle. As a fan who feels at once betrayed and yet still committed, I shall go on a diet of unsalted crackers and senna-pod tea ('Have you got the pods? Yes, but they're clearing up nicely') until I have followed you back to gauntness.

Now that we've reached page 2, let me get to my primary reason for writing, which is to ask you to honor me by autographing my copy of your book **Twice Brightly**, which I have sent in a separate package and which should arrive any day now. Alas, there is no way for me to enclose return postage; I can but thank you in advance for returning it at your own expense and pledge to be your humble servant in whatever capacity seems appropriate should you visit the Washington, D.C., area or require information therefrom. As one who has listened to several Goon Shows a week for several years, I feel an affinity to you and to the Neddie character that surpasses all rational

understanding. Thank you very much for providing so much entertainment and pleasure.
Yours truly,
Dick Baker

—————— ⟡ ——————

27th September 1985

Dick Baker,
USA Archivist,
Westmoreland Road,
Falls Church,
Virginia
USA

Dear Dick,
Many thanks for your letter and the most impressive and comprehensive list of shows etc. I've ever seen on the subject!!! It's a good job you didn't send it by carrier pigeon, it would have been in the drink just past Cape Cod! If you ever decide to part with your number plate, I could promise it a good home
Stop, stop with the stuffing of food ... that is 'out' these days. Being sylph-like is all the rage, partly because when you stand sideways, no-one can see you!! It's a pleasure to autograph your book and pay the postage ... seriously, folks!
Much love
Harry Secombe
alias Neddy Seagoon.

—————— ⟡ ——————

October 31, 1985

Dear Ned of Wales,
Allow me to add my own voice to the many other sur-
vivors of the 'Weekend Called Fred' Goon appreciation
convention in Bournemouth who are expressing their
gratitude at finally having met you in the flesh – even
though there is much less of it than in the glory days.

I had only a brief chance to mash your mitt and say
hello as you re-entered the hall on that momentous
Saturday, so I didn't get to tell you of a most remark-
able coincidence that had transpired but days before.
On the previous weekend I had viewed an obscure
movie that popped up at 4:30 in the morning on a new
cable channel, called 'Turner Classic Movies,' from the
Great Ted Turner Empire of Atlanta, Georgia and
Jane, Fonda. The movie, of which I had never thereto-
fore heard, was called – brace those monkey-ridden
knees, Ned; they could wobble at this news – Davy.

I was even more amazed to learn that the movie has
ever since been tied up in copyright in England and
that nobody in GSPS has a copy. Immediately upon
my return I mailed the tape back to London; you can
bet that it will be a highlight at the next GSPS con-
vention, although that may be twenty years from now.
Let me be the first to invite you to that event: What
the hell, George Burns has been booked into the
London Palladium for an appearance on his 100th
birthday for at least twenty years, and it looks like
he'll make it. You can make a similar commitment,
can't you?

15th November 1985

Dear Mr Baker,
Thank you for your letter dated 31st October.
I, in fact, made Davy *in 1956 and hoped that, by now, it might have disappeared.*
I believe it did well in Afghanistan where the customers were allowed to shoot at the screen!
I thoroughly enjoyed Bournemouth. I hope you did too.
My warmest wishes to you.
Sir Harry Secombe CBE

———— ✦ ————

January 29, 1989

Harry Secombe
St. James Place
London SW1

Dear Sir Harry:
You may recall my writing in the fall of 1985 and sending a photograph of my car with the enclosed license plate attached. Alas, the time has come to retire the plate from service – entirely too many local policemen and state troopers have become familiar with it. Her father spotted it too.
You would do me a great honor by accepting it as a souvenir of your days as Neddie Seagoon and of the pleasure that short, fat and dreadful Neddie brought to the colonies. I doubt that the London constabulary would let you mount it to one of your fleet of Rolls-Royces, but it might look good mounted over a basement bar.

Wishing you all the best, I remain
Your revolting servant,
Dick Baker

———— ∽◦∾ ————

9th February 1989

Dick Baker Esq.,
Westmoreland Road,
Falls Church,
Virginia

Dear Dick,
What can I say!!! Your present is wonderful. As I do
not even have one Rolls Royce let alone a fleet, it can't
go on there. I will just have to have a basement dug
under my house to put in a basement bar over which
to mount the plate!!!! Seriously folks, I will find a
suitable place, never fear. How can you bear to part
with it?? I send you Goonish greetings from this side
of the big pond!
Yours as ever,
Harry Secombe
Alias Ned of Wales.

———— ∽◦◡◦∾ ————

Rick Wakeman

Described in The Guinness Encyclopaedia of Popular
Music *as 'one of rock's premier musicians', Rick was a
superstar in the late sixties as a member of the legendary
band Yes. Since then, not only has he been voted the
world's top keyboard player innumerable times, but his solo
albums have sold millions, and his sell-out tours attract
audiences from around the world. Here, Rick remembers an
offstage moment with Harry.*

I hadn't been playing golf for very long (eight weeks to be
precise), and so I was not quite ready for my first Ryder Cup
appearance. In fact I was appalling. I knew what the problem was. I stood too close to the ball ... usually after I'd just
hit it! A thirty-yard drive off the tee was not uncommon. A
thirty-yard drive off the tee in the right direction was.

I was well aware that there was quite a large celebrity golf
circuit and was therefore not too surprised when out of the
blue, an invitation arrived in the post to take part in a
celebrity golf tournament at Effingham Golf Club. I immediately telephoned a 'celebrity' friend of mine who I knew
played in such events, to ask him what the ropes were for
the day. I had surmised that it would be relatively hilarious,
golf balls and clubs flying around all over the place.

Wrong.

My friend told me that most of the celebrities who
played had very low handicaps. (I didn't even have one
then, apart from a rotten swing.) He also told me that it
was taken very seriously.

'What's your handicap?' he enquired.

'What's the maximum allowed?' I replied.

'Twenty-eight,' said he.

'Twenty-eight then,' said I.

After putting the telephone down, I read the invitation more clearly. It was actually the Harry Secombe Golf Tournament.

Harry Secombe. One of my all-time heroes. I sat back in my chair and reminisced over those hours spent listening to the Goons as well as marvelling at Harry's wonderful voice, which was still constantly to be heard on both television and radio.

And I was possibly going to meet the great man.

And he was possibly going to watch me try and hit a golf ball.

I dialled the telephone number on the invitation in order to explain that I had only been playing a very short while, was rubbish, but loved Harry Secombe. I offered to back out.

They rejected my offer out of hand and said Harry wouldn't hear of it.

'Harry wouldn't hear of it ...' I nearly fell off my chair.

I practised really hard throughout the remaining days leading up to the tournament and reached a standard just fractionally above rubbish. When the big day came, I set off for Effingham with the golf clubs and trolley in the boot and my autograph book in my pocket.

On arrival I was greeted by Harry, who to his credit had absolutely no idea who I was but shook my hand as if I were a very dear friend. Harry has this knack with everybody and it is a real gift.

He watched my attempt to tee off. I had about eleven swipes at the ball before connecting and sending it hurtling down the fairway about thirty-five yards. Well, I had been practising to get the extra length.

'Braver man than me,' said Harry, who I now realized was not actually playing but had put the tournament together in order to raise much-needed money for a children's charity.

He greeted me again when I finished on the eighteenth. I was twenty-six balls lighter, I had lost a five-iron and was seriously considering taking up alcohol again.

'Good round?' he enquired, with that famous Secombe smile.

'Not bad,' I replied while picking the ball out of the hole after scoring an eleven.

The team I had been playing with looked at me in stunned amazement. I must have been the worst player they'd ever seen.

'Thanks for supporting us,' said Harry.

I walked away, still stunned that the great man had actually spoken to me. He was everything I had hoped he would be. Generous, kind-hearted, caring and humble.

I drove home minus twenty-six balls, one five-iron and Harry's autograph. In my schoolboy excitement I had forgotten to ask him for the very thing I wanted out of the day – so if you happen to read this, Harry ...

Dana

Irish Eurovision Song Contest winner Dana Rosemary Scallon is now an MEP, but remembers her friendship with Harry.

I can't quite place my first meeting with Sir Harry Secombe, but it was sometime in the early seventies, perhaps when I was a guest on one of his BBC TV variety shows. However, I'll always remember the introduction he gave me: 'Ladies and gentlemen, when my next guest visits Wales, she'll be sure of a Welcome on the Hillsides – they won't let her in

133

the house!' I was reduced to laughter like everyone else – a wicked Welsh plot to sabotage my song!

Soon after that memorable meeting, I was introduced to the Goons by my agent Dick Katz. Dick had been the pianist with the Ray Ellington quartet, the resident group on all the *Goon Show* radio series.

I was soon addicted to Bluebottle, Eccles, Major Bloodnok and in particular, Harry Secombe as Neddy Seagoon! An instant pick-me-up. To this day, a quick burst of the Goons and the world is a brighter, if madder place. I've been inspired by this gentleman, and Harry Secombe truly is a gentle man. His name conjures up for me a beam-ing smile, a manic laugh, that magnificent singing voice and a deep quiet faith. It's good to know you.

Michael Aspel

The man behind the famous red book first saw Harry earlier than most of us, and certainly long before This is Your Life *came on to our screens.*

We've all been aware of Harry for some time, but I first went to see him at the Windmill performing alongside Bentine when I was a schoolboy. I think I won an English award and the prize was some theatre tickets and that was one of the shows I chose to see. It was Harry's astonishing noises that I vividly recall as having the most effect on me. I've never known a comic with an easier fallback than being able to blow a raspberry at the end. He was a most endearing character then and that must have been fifty years ago.

The Summer of the Seventeenth Doll was an Australian play I enjoyed about a group of lads who used to cut sugar cane for nine months of the year. The other three months they would go down to Sydney and have a great time, and take this mannequin with them. On the seventeenth summer it all went wrong and ended. It reminds me of when years later Harry invited me to play with him at Sutton Cricket Club, opposite his house in Cheam. It was a charity team that Harry put together, and we did it for seventeen years. It was one of the highlights of my life and provided a carefree time of fun and laughter. After the seventeenth year it ended, because Harry either moved or was unwell, and I was really sad.

Harry was always there, and he used to invite people back to his house after the match. One day he showed the more serious side of himself and talked about books. He loves the use of words. We talked about certain books and he got very excited and said he had some books he knew I would like. He came downstairs with a great armful of books to give to me, and I was so thrilled and flattered and moved, but unfortunately I got so drunk that night that I forgot to take them with me!

It was such a joy to surprise him again on *This is Your Life* during his book signing in Kingston. I knew he wouldn't be able to stifle the cry of 'You've done me already!' The recent *Night of a Thousand Lives* was a wonderful evening and when they told me Harry had arrived and was in his dressing room, I went straight down to say hello. The amazing thing about Harry is that he makes you think you are the one person he would most like to see. He struggled up out of his chair – no, actually leapt really – and embraced me. When he made his entrance on stage there was uproar as all the other guests gave him a standing ovation because he is so loved.

Modern comedians today are respected and admired, but not loved. There are a lot of clever, very amusing people around, but once they're off the screen or have left the stage you don't give them another thought. You think of Harry and you smile. There is a warmth from Harry that never dims. It's a rather old-fashioned quality, I suppose. It's a species that is becoming extinct.

What makes me laugh is seeing him amused and made so happy by what he is doing. Apart from his singing talent, if you analyse his humour, it's a series of schoolboy, 'not grown up' type of noises. It appeals because it makes us feel young and silly again.

In his maturer years I felt he sang much better than in the early days, when it seemed he sang a little bit sharp. He was then smack on the note, and what a gift! I suppose there is a Welshman who is unable to sing, though I can't say I've met him yet. Except, of course, they don't all sing as well as Harry. When people used to say, why doesn't he stop doing the comedy and just sing, it was silly even to consider it. It would be like asking Harry to cut himself in half.

Unlike many performers, Harry has lasted the test of time and still appears even when he's been unwell. It's nothing to do with sentimentality, but real affection. There are people who probably do cleverer comedy, there might be those who sing better, but nobody has the personality and that infectious quality that makes you smile. I will always remember Harry as the one who came towards me with his arms open in every sense, personally and in performance.

It is true that 'age cannot dim', because when I see Harry now, I still see that silly bloke on stage at the Windmill. It's amazing to think that my youngest son Daniel is the same age as I was when I saw Harry at the Windmill, and is himself a great fan of the Goons. They obviously have a whole new generation of admirers.

Marian Montgomery and Laurie Holloway

As a couple collectively known as one of the best jazz duos around today, Marian has enjoyed a successful career with her albums and live performances, and Laurie can be seen beaming from behind the piano on the BBC's Parkinson.

Needless to say, our admiration for Harry is palpable and the respect in which we hold him is enormous. Specifically we admire his honesty and the way in which he has conducted his life both in and out of the business. I don't think anyone can find superlatives enough to comment on his sense of humour and timing. It is just a pleasure to be around while he is around and to enjoy the benefits of his work.

Gary Wilmot

Now known as a major musical star, when he first worked with Harry he was part of a new double act, Gary Wilmot and Judy. They had won the television talent show New Faces *and one of their first bookings was to support an ex-Goon.*

Sitting as part of that amazingly star-studded audience during the BBC's *Night of a Thousand Lives*, I felt the atmosphere go from relaxed to electric when Harry Secombe entered as special guest. It was quite an emotional moment as he chatted away to Michael Aspel, and many memories of my own came flooding back.

As a new act I was in awe of his arrival at the theatre, and wasn't to be disappointed. As his huge 'HS1' number-plated Rolls Royce pulled up, I noticed that he was the

137

only one to be allowed to park on the forecourt of the theatre. On that cold and drizzly Sunday afternoon, the rest of us had walked from the multi-storey down the road. Never mind, I thought, he is the star.

When Harry emerged from the car, I could almost feel the loveliness of the man's reputation get out with him. His graciousness matched the size of the car and the size of his belt, as he greeted me like a long-lost friend, even though it was the first time I had ever met him. Suddenly, a chilly Sunday afternoon began to warm up as we chatted with the man that I had heard so much about. There are only two other star names that have been so welcoming to me in the same way, Mike and Bernie Winters and dear Roy Castle.

I can't remember how long he stood there bubbling away, blowing raspberries and raising his eyebrows, but it seemed forever. He was in no hurry to rush off into a dressing room and close the door like some of our colleagues.

Having done my piece on stage, I stood in the wings to see how the master would do it. Having listened to the Goons as a young boy at home, I really hadn't understood their type of anarchic humour, but I was content just to listen to the sound of the laughter it produced elsewhere. Radio comedy was instrumental in my determination to make people laugh.

It's true that many comedians originally used their skill in making people laugh to escape from their environment; perhaps they were running from something, or trying to cover something up, or they came from a very poor background. For me it was the fact that I was the only black boy in my community. Maybe comedy was a child's way for me to say that I was as good as everyone else, because I could make them all laugh. It seemed to work and I stuck at it. Now I'm glad I did, and I'm grateful to folk like Harry who pioneered the pathway of comedy for others like me to follow.

Jimmy Cricket

*With a management called Wellie Boot Productions, and the
onstage costume to match, Jimmy Cricket is immediately
recognizable as one of the UK's funniest character comedians.*

What can you say about Sir Harry, from the legendary
Goon Show on steam radio when the family used to sit
round listening and picturing those surreal characters in
their heads, to West End blockbuster musicals like *Pickwick*,
where his beautiful voice would enthral audiences?

Sir Harry has that all-round talent given only to a few.
Add to this the fact he is one of nature's gentlemen and
you have a true star.

Joan Morecambe and Doreen Wise

*Remembered as the most successful and best-loved double-
act of all time, Morecambe and Wise attracted a television
audience of twenty-eight million viewers for their renowned
Christmas show of 1977. Throughout their long career, Eric
and Ernie maintained and increased their popularity year
after year and still remain at the top of the television ratings
many years later. Their wives, Joan and Doreen, remember
how much the boys loved working with Harry.*

We both remember fond and happy times spent with
Harry and Myra, but with the peculiarities of show business, all too often our families seemed to pass like ships in
the night. Pantomimes and summer seasons were a chance
to cement relationships and our best memory is during a
season of *Puss in Boots* in Coventry.

We all considered Harry a very funny fellow, and one night he proved it after the finale when he picked up Eric and Ernie and placed one under each arm. He then proceeded to carry them both off stage, flying past the wings and down into the corridor, laughing all the way to the dressing room.

They had many laughs together backstage and made all the long and cramped hours spent in the theatre bearable. Harry was a dear friend.

Ronnie Barker

Open All Hours, Porridge, The Two Ronnies – *what more can one say about one of the country's most loved funny-men? Ronnie has appeared on TV and stage for more than fifty years, and holds the distinction of being the writer of the country's favourite sketch: 'Fork 'andles'.*

Harry Secombe has contributed to the world of comedy a tremendous and infectious sense of joyousness.

He enters a room, talks and laughs with people, and when he leaves that room, people are invariably happier than they were. (Harry would say, 'Of course they are. They're glad to see the back of me!') He has giggled his way into millions of people's hearts.

I have only worked with him once. I say worked, we laughed much more than we rehearsed. Those were the days, of course, when we were both drinking men. (Harry interrupts: 'That's a lie! I never drank men, I drank beer.')

We first met at the palatial mansion of Mickie Most, the music man. After a very large and fairly wet lunch, we prepared to leave. Harry stood on the vast steps at the front of the house, surrounded by giant pillars, a perfect stage set. He went down on one knee, à la Jolson, and sang:

> *I'd walk a million miles*
> *If I hadn't got piles*
> *My Ma-ha-ha-hammy!*

I love him as everyone else loves him, dearly.

Cleo Laine

Celebrated across the world as a singer with a fascinating voice, Cleo has often bumped into Harry in different parts of the globe.

Perth holds good memories of our encounter with Harry Secombe, who made regular visits, creating warmth, mayhem, fun and laughter in seconds at any press conference he attended. Johnny Franz, Harry's long-time pianist (and my early A & R man at Fontana Records) told of arriving late to do a concert with Harry as his car had broken down. He apologized profusely to Harry while at the same time cursing his darned Rolls Royce for letting him down. In mock effrontery Harry, pulling himself up to his full, Welsh, defensive height, said to Johnny: 'A Rolls Royce does not break down, it just declines to proceed.'

Ray Norwood

Family celebrations have always been important to Harry, and his old artillery pal was one of the first to send a card on the occasion of Harry and Myra's golden wedding.

Once upon a time in the land of laver bread
The Mumbles train, Kieft the chemist,
Baldwin's Wind Street and Eynon's pies,
Family Secombe begat a son
And the family Atherton begat a daughter
And it came to pass that there was a coming together
* of the two begats*
Thence a bond in holy wedlock.
Early days, lean times
But as time passeth
Clouds breaketh
And in the fullness of time they achieve great fame.
Conquering that fame and making the nice unspoiled
* couple they are today*
Equally at home with beggar or king.

Showman Secombe

A comic has to be an actor. You've got to pretend to be funny and happy whatever happens.

HARRY SECOMBE

It was actor Edward Woodward who stood up at the late Les Dawson's memorial service in Westminster Abbey and announced that comedians are the most underrated people in our society. What would life be like, he went on to say, if we hadn't got those people who brought such colour into the greyness of our lives?

'We go through our nine-to-five lives, face pressure at work, then come back home to our families and their problems, so how wonderful it is to see laughter help us to relax. What richness these people bring to our lives. Comedians earn every penny they get,' added another speaker.

Above a small pub in Grays Inn Road, London is located one of the homes of laughter – The Water Rats. A well-established show business charity that raises money through shows every year, its members are proud that Harry is one of them. On its walls, among photos of famous variety performers down the years such as Flanagan and Allen, Dickie Henderson, Laurel and Hardy and Max Miller, sits Harry's picture, beaming out from a collage of major stars.

Harry began his charity work quietly, and long ago, as his award in 1963 of a CBE illustrates. His knighthood in 1981 was one of the proudest moments of his life, although as he joked to the press at the time, he wondered if Buckingham Palace had called him in to take the CBE back!

But The Water Rats are not the only charity to which Harry has given his efforts. He has taken up every possible opportunity to help out, and sometimes it has cost him a lot of effort. Treating every show with equal value, Harry has always given one hundred per cent at his charity appearances. On one occasion, following two panto performances, he agreed to do a midnight charity matinee. On stage Harry did his knockabout routine, followed by two arias. 'When he came off I could see he was absolutely soaked in sweat,' reports Doone Ellerton, who was in the show with Harry. 'I was a bit worried at how ill he looked for a moment, and wondered if he had been overdoing things. I asked him if he was all right, but he just smiled and said, "I think I should have done the arias first, Doone!"'

The Harry Secombe Golf Classic, first played in 1967, has raised more than £250,000 for the physically and mentally disabled. Lord Rix remembers that it was Harry's name which brought new standards to charity golf tournaments, explaining that previous events had often foundered because the amount raised hardly covered the running expenses.

'There is one golf classic – that named after Sir Harry Secombe – which has gone on for years and years and always increases its take for the lucky recipients, the Lord's Taverners,' says Brian. 'Now the Lord's Taverners started life in 1950 when a bunch of theatricals, headed by Martin

Boddey, John Mills (before his knighthood), Michael Shepley, Stephen Mitchell, John Snagge, as well as some others, decided that as they spent a great deal of time watching cricket in front of the Tavern at Lord's it would be a good idea to club together to do something, in return, for cricket. And that's where the money went at first, to youth cricket, as well as to the National Playing Fields Association, when the Duke of Edinburgh became the patron and twelfth man. Mind you, there wasn't much money, but it was a start.

'Gradually the group expanded, to include prominent businessmen as well as famous actors and cricketers, but the numbers have always been kept down to around 750, although there are many more Friends in the regions. Originally, the money was raised by charity cricket matches and, eventually, a ball. Then the Harry Secombe Classic was added, followed by rugger and numerous social events. Such was the income that a Foundation Committee was formed (on which I serve) and the funds distributed by us in the ratio of 45 per cent to youth cricket and 55 per cent to help disabled young people, both in leisure pursuits and the general day-to-day problems of living. In 1987–8 we reached our first million pounds for the year and celebrated by awarding five other charities £5,000 each for unusually helpful work in the field of leisure, with an additional £500 for five handicapped individuals whose personal achievement was outstanding. This in one year alone, plus forty-two coaches for disabled people (known as New Horizons) and the balance of £829,469 being distributed in grant aid for all those we can help. Not bad for a bunch of rogues and vagabonds who only went along for the beer and remained to provide champagne!'

It is normal for any show business name to have a favourite charity to which they give time and energy in fundraising events and shows. Harry, as usual, is different. For him, one is never enough. He has, to give one further example, raised more than three million pounds for war widows and orphans. The numerous causes for which he has worked so hard over the years also include the Army Benevolent Fund, the Variety Club Of Great Britain, the British Diabetic Society, Stars Organization for Spastics, the Friends of St Helier Hospital and Cancer Research, to name but a few.

He was even active in writing to newspapers in order to engender greater support for the concerns he held, as his recent letter to several newspapers about cancer illustrates:

> *I am writing to you with a personal plea to help save lives.*
>
> *June is the Cancer Research Campaign's Men's Cancer Awareness Month and the charity is particularly focusing on prostate cancer – the second most common cancer in men in Britain.*
>
> *This disease claims the lives of nearly 10,000 British men every year and as with most forms of cancer, early diagnosis is crucial for the best chance of survival.*
>
> *I should know. I was diagnosed with prostate cancer myself after going to see my GP because I was experiencing abdominal pain.*
>
> *It is two years since my diagnosis and I am still undergoing treatment ...'*

Cancer Research is particularly close to his heart, not just because he has experienced cancer first hand, but also because he has seen its effect on the lives of many of his friends, not least his old friend Roy Castle. *Pickwick*, Roy's last show, which gave him the opportunity to leave us with a truly memorable performance, also vividly demonstrated life's twists and turns and the way in which things connect. It was significant not just because it was the show that gave Harry greater pleasure than any other in which he has performed, nor just because it toured the USA with great success or enjoyed a long West End run, providing work for many individuals and pleasure for thousands. In Fiona Castle's eyes there is a simple but precious reason to be grateful for that show.

'It was during *Pickwick* that Harry cajoled Roy into writing his autobiography, and rang his own publisher in order to start the ball rolling,' explains Fiona. 'Within two days the publisher had been down to see him and Roy had started writing his life story. The publisher gave Roy a tight deadline, for June,' recalls Fiona. 'If they had given him a later deadline, the book would never have been finished. I'm grateful to Harry for that, and for the fact that I have such a wonderful reminder of Roy. I'm sure I would have forgotten most of the stories.'

In fact it was Harry's idea to do *Pickwick* in the first place, the idea first coming to him while he was on holiday in Barbados.

Until the early sixties, Harry had done most of his shows for impresario Bernard Delfont. The Palladium seasons were all Delfont productions, as were *The Plumber's Progress* and *The Four Musketeers*, which followed much later. Bernard was an impresario who loved the theatre and all the people in it, and took great pride in looking after his array of stars, none more so than Harry. He booked Harry as often as possible at his top venue, the London Palladium.

The Palladium remains a byword for entertainment excellence around the world, and a performance there represents the 'coming of age' of any hopeful celebrity. Once the Palladium is on your CV you have a stamp of authority that says you've arrived. For Harry the Palladium itself was always the star and he soaked up its atmosphere like any other performer. The Palladium is known as one of the most professionally run venues in the country, and remarkably, a number of its staff have been there for more than thirty years. Its resident orchestra was the best in the business; it was conducted by Eric Rogers, who created the famous Palladium theme tune. Harry enjoyed Eric's sense of humour and marvelled at the fact that he could step off the conductor's platform and play any instrument in the pit. He was to write a lot of the music for the *Carry On* films, and eventually the orchestrations of *Oliver!* for Harry. The Palladium also enjoyed its own chaplain, Guy Bennett, for over twenty-five years.

The backstage Number One dressing room was always prepared and decorated to the personal taste and requirements of its user. Yul Brynner was said to have spent £50,000 of his own money transforming this dressing room when he brought his show *The King and I* to town. It was Max Bygraves who had the pleasure of being the next star to use the now sumptuous room.

Harry would make this room into a 'home from home', a place into which he felt he could invite others when they called backstage to see him. He shared the room in typical Harry fashion. When American artists came over to work at the venue, they were always eager to sample the ambience of the Number One dressing room, and were disappointed if they found it was already occupied. On several occasions, Harry would dress in the corridor outside while his American friends gleefully indulged themselves in his room.

Harry was to play this salubrious venue many times. He was usually happier appearing in his own runs, rather than one-offs such as the Royal Variety Performances, which because of their scale were always very stressful productions.

When friends were on the bill, however, it was always of special delight to him. Norman Vaughan was invited to compere the Royal Variety Show in 1962 in the presence of Her Majesty Queen Elizabeth II and the Duke of Edinburgh. Norman was particularly pleased that Harry was on the bill along with Eartha Kitt, Cliff Richard, Frank Ifield, Bob Hope and many others. It was an extraordinary show with such a strong array of talent and with Norman at the helm, as impresario Lord Delfont remembers:

The Queen and Prince Philip were treated to an evening of non-stop entertainment at the Palladium. There was fine singing from two female vocalists who have delighted audiences for many years now, Eartha Kitt and Cleo Laine, comedy from Norman Vaughan as compere, from Mike and Bernie Winters, and Dickie Henderson, while a surprise hit was the astounding juggling of Rudy Cardenas.

The end of the show belonged to the Americans. First came Sophie Tucker in an emotional appearance: a hard act to follow, but who can upstage Bob Hope? The master of comedy soon had the audience fully with him and, aided by Edie Adams, brought the house down.

Sophie Tucker, 'The Last of the Red Hot Mommas', was given a huge ovation at the 1962 show. She was overwhelmed but knew it was a fitting tribute. 'I worked forty years for this night and I reckon I've earned it. It was in 1922 that I made my first appearance in a Royal Variety Show. Tonight they loved it, they loved it, they loved it. The Queen and the Prince were wonderful to me. We had some good laughs together.'

Eartha Kitt was disconcerted by being told not to look at the Queen during her act. Ms Kitt had hoped

*to direct her song at the Royal Box when uttering the
words 'Would you think it a bore if I showed you the
door?'*

*'I'm disappointed I can't look at the Royal Box as I
sing,' she said. 'I like to bring people into my act, but
it seems it is just not done here. It's not a naughty
song – I don't sing naughty songs.'*

The show was such a success that Norman was invited to
take over from Bruce Forsyth, who was taking a break from
the immensely popular television show *Sunday Night at the
London Palladium*. Norman went on to do the show for
three years, but when he was first booked he was told not
to tell anyone. It was impossible for Norman to keep totally
'mum' for over three months, so he decided the one person
he would let in on the secret would be Harry, knowing he
could be trusted implicitly.

'Two months before the show started, I knew I must tell
Harry,' says Norman. 'He lived in Sutton at the time, and I
lived down the road in Carshalton, so it was easy for me to
see him. By the time I arrived at his front door, I was very
nervous and agitated. It must have shown, because when
Harry invited me in, I could see that he was getting a little
worried.

'I asked if we could go into his study as I had something
very important to say, but it would have to be in private.
Harry, now looking a little more concerned, ushered me
through to the back and sat silently to await whatever I
had to say.

'"Harry," I started apprehensively, "I want you to know
that ... I've got the job at the Palladium!"

'Harry nearly fell off his chair with the shock. "That's
wonderful, marvellous," he smiled. Then with a big sigh of
relief, "I had a bit of a fright," he said. "I thought for a

minute you were going to ask for my daughter's hand in marriage!"'

Outside the realm of live theatre, after nearly ten years of the Goons, the gang had decided that they had gone as far as they could. It seemed that they had spent their entire time together exploding one another. And not only had they blown up everything in sight – somehow every time they lit a match a Doodlebug was launched across the Channel which blew up Min and Hen's legs, Bluebottle and Eccles were continually scraped off the wall after being placed in a cannon, or Moriarty enjoyed a nice long cigar with a fuse on the end of it – but a whole 'Goonology' had been launched. Over the years hundreds of books were to be published, some seriously trying to decipher the meaning of the comedy, others taking each episode apart like a mechanic stripping down a car: books such as *The Goon Show Companion*, *The Story of the Goons*, *The Goon Show Scripts*, *More Goon Show Scripts*, *The Book of Goons*, *The Lost Goon Shows*, and *The Last Goon Show of All*.

Bentine, Sellers, Milligan and Secombe had all developed successful solo careers and each of them was keen to spend more time reaching his full potential. Millions had grown up on *The Goon Show* and its comedy, even if some of those described it as total inanity. Many people listen to the radio either to be moved or to escape; with the Goons it was total escapism, and was wonderfully received. A few listeners were too serious to appreciate it, like the man at the BBC who called it the 'Go-On Show'; the rest simply lapped it up. With the broadcast on 28 January 1960 of the last *Goon Show*, an historic chapter was at an end. But for Harry a new one was about to begin.

The Goons now behind him, and having topped the bill at the London Palladium in his own show five times within five years, Harry knew he was facing a professional dilemma. He felt he had explored every available opportunity, so where should he go from here? Perhaps, he thought, he should create a new pathway for himself.

It was the front cover of the Christmas edition of the *TV Times* that was to inspire him. Staring at himself dressed as Father Christmas advertising a seasonal programme, Harry remembered that he had played the part of a Dickensian innkeeper in the same show, and over lunch mentioned to Wolf Mankowitz the idea of playing the leading character from *The Pickwick Papers* which had occurred to him on holiday in Barbados. Wolf offered to do the adaptation and Harry's idea snowballed from then on, with Leslie Bricusse writing the score and Bernard Delfont producing. Its opening night was at the Palace Theatre, Manchester on 3 June 1963. It was a huge success and eventually transferred to London's Saville Theatre in Shaftesbury Avenue for two years. Harry sang the song 'If I Ruled the World' each night almost as if he did. One would imagine that if he really did rule the world, it would indeed be a better place to live in.

Bernard Delfont was keen to take the show abroad and in 1965 negotiated with the American impresario David Merrick to take the show to the States. The show toured San Francisco, Los Angeles, Cleveland, Detroit and Washington before arriving on Broadway. Despite a very successful out-of-town run, the 'Butchers Of Broadway', as the New York critics are known, pulled it to bits, and it closed within weeks.

'One of the funniest images I have of *Pickwick* is not the show itself,' recalls Fiona Castle, 'but is to do with the nomination for the Tony awards it received. The show had closed the previous year and had been panned by the critics, yet had made a lot of money at the box office. The critics have a lot of power on Broadway and it seems

that simply on a matter of opinion and taste a whole company can go under, putting everyone out of work within
days.

'Harry and his company had completed a flourishing
tour of the USA, yet the Broadway run lasted only three
weeks. The saving grace was the Tony nomination, for
which Harry and Roy travelled back to New York a year
later, hoping to receive the award and bring it back
proudly to England. It was not to be.

'There they were at the awards ceremony,' laughs Fiona,
'standing in a corner looking all misplaced because nobody
there knew them. To give themselves some confidence they
began singing "If I Ruled the World" to themselves, but no
one looked up from their pleasantries. This picture of all
the big American stars milling around and greeting each
other while Harry and Roy stood there looking like two
little lost boys makes me laugh out loud whenever I think
of it. It was Laurel and Hardy all over again.'

When Roy was diagnosed with cancer, Harry was one of
the first people he telephoned. 'I was standing beside Roy
when he made that call,' remembers Fiona. 'He had only
just got the words out about his condition when Harry
burst into tears and put the phone down. A few moments
later he called back and apologized to Roy for not being
able to cope with the news.'

Within a week of the telephone call the Secombes went
to see Roy and Fiona at home. 'All I can remember about
that day was that we spent the whole time laughing,'
smiles Fiona. 'It was such good therapy for Roy.

'Our son Daniel arrived later that day from Norway
with his girlfriend, and soon-to-be wife, who is Norwegian,
and had never heard of Harry Secombe. Gertha sat staring
at this mad family rolling around in fits and wondering
what on earth she was doing there!

'It's typical of Harry to be able to generate that sort of fun, even in the most difficult of times. Whenever he and Roy got together after that it was just one gag, and one reminiscence after another. It was the best medicine that Roy could have had.'

Roy himself records how Harry played host on many occasions.

> Next day, Harry Secombe's driver collected us and we enjoyed a great day with him and his brood. It was a beautiful May Day and the sprawling lawns were so peaceful, with unspoilt views almost to the Sussex coast. I tried to play cricket with Harry's grandchildren, which made me realize how totally out of shape I was. It was very funny as I bent down to 'snatch' a ball which had passed me ten seconds ago.
>
> We wandered around the big garden and budding fruit trees as more memories flooded back. Harry told me of the possibility of resurrecting Pickwick sometime in the future. I had been his Sam Weller on Broadway twenty-eight years ago. More precious memories. I dared not even consider that I would be a small part of it at this time – so I didn't!
>
> After being fed luxuriously – twice – we piled back into his limo and were smoothed home. We were in a happy, dreamy state of euphoria – until we discovered our oil-fired boiler had burst and water was trickling gaily down the path!

'It's strange to say,' explains Fiona. 'But Roy and I laughed more during the time of his illness than at any other time in our marriage. When I first saw Eric, Harry and Roy performing, I decided then that I wanted to marry a man who could make me laugh. Laughter is so valuable, brings healing and reconciliation and provides such a wonderful atmosphere to live in, even in the middle of adversity. Harry enabled Roy to laugh at his illness rather than allow it to defeat him. The funniest things are often the things that go wrong, and there are a lot of incidents that I still look back on and giggle over. Laughter has helped me to come to terms with Roy's death, and I thank Harry for his part in that.'

For the final tour of *Pickwick*, Harry asked Roy, his cancer temporarily in remission, to take part once again. Despite Roy's illness, Harry was amazed that it seemed impossible to tell anything was wrong from seeing him on stage. It was only afterwards, upon passing Roy's dressing room in the backstage corridor, that Harry became aware of the cost, when he noticed Roy flat out on the floor, trying to recover.

When it was time for the curtain calls at the end of the show, Harry would make Roy take the central bow each night. It drew a tremendous reception from the audience, who would stand on their feet in an outpouring of love for the man and in gratitude for a great performance. Harry, big enough to take second place to his pal each night, stood by Roy's side as he looked around wondering what he had done to deserve such a response.

Harry was at his holiday home in Majorca when Roy rang him one day. As he listened to Roy explain that he was phoning to say hello for the last time, it was unearthly difficult for Harry to take in his words. After a joke or two, Roy went on to explain that he was about to take a course of medication that would prevent him from being able to talk properly any more. Harry was stunned, speechless, as he listened to Roy, who refused to say goodbye but simply said, 'I'll see you, Harry!' Harry put the phone down and couldn't have felt emptier or sadder.

Harry was now aware of his own age and mortality. In his autobiography a lot of the deep emotions within him are typically played down. Although not utterly self-effacing, he is not one to make a fuss over himself. While in Australia, already suffering from peritonitis, he was diagnosed with diabetes. In his book he hardly mentions this and makes no comment on his own feelings, and yet he must have been secretly terrified. 'Diabetes is a lifelong scourge,' says Fiona Castle. 'You don't ever get cured of that, you just have to live with it through drugs and injections.'

Harry merely pushed the hurdles to one side and carried on. He couldn't see a time when he would replace it all with a pair of carpet slippers. Entertainers never really retire, they just stop working either when they are too ill or their skills are no longer in demand. Harry was still enjoying the business so much that the age of sixty-five disappeared over the horizon just as quickly as it had appeared, as he carried on in all manner of roles, and increased his charity work.

But in September 1999, Harry was reported in the *South Wales Evening Post* as having made what he warned would be his last public appearance. As he launched the charity golf classic named after him, 'I won't be performing again,' he said. 'I had a stroke at the end of January, I am a diabetic and I have got prostate cancer. I am lucky to be alive!'

Although looking thin and frail, Harry was said to be as lively and irrepressible as ever at the event in Surrey, where he was surrounded by famous faces. At one point he brandished his walking stick like a golf club and shouted 'I did it Highway!' as he swung it into the air.

Actor James Bolam said: 'Harry is so loved, not just in the business as a whole, but in each part of it, as a comedian and a singer. He is a wonderful, vibrant personality.

Usually he just follows us around in his buggy, blowing raspberries.'

As Harry's health problems encouraged him to take more of a back seat, he had already begun to favour the idea of reducing the pressure of work a little, so that he could spend more time relaxing and meeting friends. Extended holidays at his home in Majorca had become more frequent, but he always looked forward to returning to his old pals. He especially loved it when he hadn't seen someone for two or three years and was able to pick up a relationship again from where it had been left off.

Harry took a similar delight in his army regiment's yearly reunions and had always attended as many as his time would allow. The final reunion took place on 4 June 2000, when forty-eight of the 250 former comrades of 132 Welsh Field Regiment returned to their old stamping ground of sixty years before. Officers of the Field Support Squadron played host to the old soldiers in an event held at the Drill Hall, Swansea, which had been the artillerymen's base before they went to war. In an emotional evening, most of the time was spent reminiscing about the old days and what had happened to members of the company since, but a few moments were reserved to reflect upon and remember those comrades killed in action. Despite his poor health, Harry was determined to make the two-hundred-mile trip. 'Sadly I haven't been able to make the last few reunions because of my illness but I wouldn't have missed this one for the world. These lads really are the salt of the earth. It is the last time we shall meet, and we are very sad,' he said at a press conference. 'It's time to call a halt. Anno Domini has beaten us, not the Germans!'

Some of his old comrades were worried that he would be making the trip in such a fragile state of health, but they had forgotten how stubborn Harry could be. Not only did he put all his strength and efforts into joining his mates but he also refused any help in reaching the top of the stairs that swept up into the dining room at their old barracks.

Sitting beside him at the banquet was Ray Norwood, his old pal from the early invasions of Algiers and Sicily. Ray had lost track of Harry some years earlier. He couldn't believe his eyes when one day he found that that same Goon-like friend was appearing on television and radio. 'Harry had just started to make his mark when I noticed he was appearing in a show at the Swansea Empire. I dropped a quick note off to him at the stage door, never really thinking it would get to this new star. He immediately sent a note back and invited my wife, Ruth, and me round to his dressing room after the show. I sat there laughing at the shaving sketch and wondered what it would be like meeting him after all these years. When we got backstage and were shown into his room, to my instant delight he was the same old Harry.

'He had just purchased his first car, an Austin Atlantic, and he invited us out for a spin. We thought we were the bee's knees in this, but Harry never played the star, he was just like an old pal. There was always a great welcome from Harry, who obviously valued his old friends, perhaps above anything else. Where I come from, men don't usually use the words "we loved him" but it's the nearest term I can use, and I still look forward to meeting him every time we get a chance to do so.'

Most old soldiers are reluctant to talk about the conflict they have experienced, perhaps for fear of bringing back terrible memories that they would rather forget. Still suffering from occasional nightmares, it was difficult for Harry to tell anyone about the dreadful times, but he found he could relive those moments among people with whom he had shared them. In its own way it's a cathartic exercise

158

to allow the memories to surface and discuss them with the boys, and in so doing to feel a little better. This is why the regimental reunions were so important to him, and why he made every effort to be at the yearly gathering in Swansea.

Quietly Harry would help some of the lads from the regiment who were going through hard times. Others approached him for help, some genuine and some perhaps not so genuine, but Harry would never turn anyone away. It was reported that he even paid the medical bills of one of his fellow Goons who had hit hard times. 'And why not?' would be Harry's response, and yet this type of generosity, gently and secretly shown, is one of Harry's hallmarks, like the stamp on the bottom of a silver spoon. It's this inner generosity that also appears onstage in his desire to give the audience everything he has.

Harry's wartime escapades and famous face had meant that he was an ideal choice to encourage the current troops as well as the veterans of war. He travelled to the Falklands, and was invited to perform at a number of military events such as the fortieth anniversary celebrations of VE Day in 1985, before being whisked abroad again just before the Gulf War.

When Harry arrived in the desert he stood watching the preparations with sadness. For he knew that the same things were about to happen that had happened to him in World War Two. Making a tour of the area, Harry looked at the huge guns waiting in readiness to be fired. The same camouflage nets, tents, groundsheets on the floor and Christmas cards nailed on the tent poles, reminded him that nothing had really changed in the fifty-odd years since he had fought. But the atmosphere was much less 'gung-ho', he noticed, with a real sense of 'let's get this job done and get back home as soon as possible' hanging in the air.

Harry's support, understanding and empathy with the Services have been invaluable. One feels that if we all took on Harry's ethos of life, there would be no need for war in the first place. As his old comrade Ray Norwood suggests, 'If we were all Harrys it would be Utopia.'

Terry Wogan

With his BBC Radio 2 morning show, which has achieved legendary status, and his hilarious epitaphs to 'Auntie's' mistakes, Terry remains one of the nation's best-loved broadcasters and presenters.

A few years ago, the Lord's Taverners decided to 'roast' Sir Harry at a special dinner. It didn't work; nobody could find a bad word to say about the old boy, even in fun. The only time I can remember even a mildly harsh criticism was on a television interview I did with Sir Harry and the Sainted Lady Myra. He'd lost weight, and I congratulated him on his snake-like aspect. 'Ah,' admonished the Light of his Life, who was sitting in as referee, 'Ah, but he's lost his sparkle ...' Since he started out with ten times the sparkle of the average firework, only a wife would have noticed. If there's a better humoured, better natured, better man around, I have yet to meet him. And that laugh, like an explosion in a laver bread factory ...

I, in common with the entire world, love and admire the man.

Jim Davidson OBE

Harry calls Jim the tearaway lad with a heart of gold. Like Harry, Jim also has a heart for those who have known the conflict of war.

People always thank me for being the first entertainer to go to the Falkland Islands to entertain British servicemen and women, and I tell them that was not the case.

The first man to the Falklands was Sir Harry Secombe, who despite having to live on Gurkha curry for ten days, gave our troops a laugh and a much-needed boost. Harry is a great bloke!

Roy Castle

Remembered by the nation as one of the finest all-round comedy entertainers of all time, Roy recalls with great affection the night when Harry made him a star.

As I walked out I was completely fazed by the magnificent Royal Box housing Her Majesty and the Duke, looking at ME. The audience also threw me, as I had never seen a huge house full, in formal dress. No one had ever mentioned this; it was a wonderful but awesome sight. Time to sing as the conductor looked at me expectantly – 'The whole town's talkin' about the Jones boy' – I remembered the words and the trumpet sat pleasantly and the valves came back up again. Generous applause. My guitar 'bit' involved a little humour and I was one of the first to dare to guy Elvis Presley and the rock 'n' roll bunch. My remarks were centred on the three-chord trick and the gyrating hips. At one point, Prince Philip guffawed all by himself. The whole audience looked at him, then back at me and then laughed. I am certain it was that very moment which launched me into the big time.

The rest of that short routine got good laughs and my Jerry Lewis tap routine fairly sizzled. I finished to solid applause as I took a bow to the audience and one to the Royal Box and off I went in a blue haze. The other performers in the wings were all applauding as I staggered through them. I floated back towards my dressing room in a completely drained but thankful state, when Harry Secombe raced after me, grabbed my arm and dragged me back to the stage. 'Take another bow, son, they love you.' He eased me back out there and I had to take another bow to audience and Royal Box ... and Mam was out there. The little girl who won the talent competition but wasn't able to pursue her career, finally watched her son perform for royalty. Melodramatic, I know, but for me it meant everything. I was asked to join the line-up after the show and was introduced to the Royals. Whenever interviewers ask me what my greatest moment in show business was – look no further. It would not be possible to have such a big leap forward ever again. 'You shall go to the ball.'

Pickwick opened at the 46th Street Theatre during a newspaper strike. Consequently our publicity was cramped to say the least, and although the audiences were good and the show was going well, David Merrick the producer took it off after three weeks. I was so sad for the whole cast, who had pinned their hopes on a long run. Harry's Rolls Royce was halfway across the Atlantic and had to be sent straight back. However, Harry and I did get nominated for Tony awards, which was some consolation.

A few funny things happened to us during our three weeks on Broadway. Harry and I were invited to a Variety

Club lunch just before we opened. Princess Margaret was guest of honour. Lots of big American stars were there, each with their own ring of admirers clamouring around them, rather like a chrysanthemum. Each time the celebrity made a joke, the chrysanthemum would open up in gales of laughter, and then close up until the next gem.

Harry and I were on our own, more like a pair of wall-flowers. As waiters flitted by with trays full of aperitifs we would just be about to take one when the tray went straight by us. After a few minutes of this, Harry looked at me, a wicked twinkle in his eye. He took a deep breath and, at the top of his voice, bellowed 'If I ruled the world.' Every chrysanthemum turned and stared at us, for two seconds ... then realized we were nobody and turned back again. The drinks waiters still flashed by us.

Dickie Henderson

In a career spanning fifty years Dickie Henderson worked his way up from prop boy to become one of the country's most successful stage and television artists. Here he recalls the early years of life with Harry.

Nightclub work was terrifying at first. To get the job I did an audition to a late night/early morning audience. These unsuspecting souls saw job-seeking 'triers' working for free. I once saw Harry Secombe bite the dust there through sheer nerves. He worked so fast he sounded like a tape recorder going backwards.

On our trips we had many weird flights in light aircraft. I'll never forget one in a lightning storm, flying in a single-engined plane from North Devon with Harry Secombe and Roy Castle, the radio packing up just as we were landing back at Blackbushe. The brave pilot, who must have been getting messages from Biggles, decided to land by the seat of his pants. All that was missing from his uniform was a leather helmet and a white scarf.

Approaching the runway we saw the murky outline of a figure waving frantically. This we construed as a warning not to land. The controls were pulled back and we overshot the runway, missing the rooftops by too close a margin for comfort; a quick turn round the aerodrome and we were guided on to the adjoining runway. Alighting, we were then informed that the original runway was flooded and that if we had landed we would have bought our lot. We just smiled weakly and said cheerio.

Harry is amazing; he's spent his entire working life in this very competitive business and never put a foot wrong. I can't imagine Harry falling out with anybody.

Grahame Laurence

Musical director Grahame remembers a moment of tension defused by Harry.

The number of artistes on the bill for a Royal Variety Performance in the mid-eighties necessitated sharing dressing rooms; Harry was sharing with Mike Yarwood, for whom I was musical director at the time.

I was in the dressing room with Mike when Harry came off stage from his performance. He walked in, admired himself in the full-length mirror, giggled, and said, 'Well, Harry, you got away with it again!'

John Cleese

Both the name and the face behind such comedy classics as Fawlty Towers *and* Monty Python, *John's contribution to comedy is immeasurable. Here he pays tribute to a fellow laughter maker.*

I worked with Harry several times back in the middle of the eighteenth century and I think he is one of the nicest, kindest and most entertaining human beings I have ever met.

I have admired him ever since I was an obsessed fan of *The Goon Show* as a schoolboy, and even then I realized how he held that show together as a performer. With Milligan and Sellers doing all those amazing voices, it needed a warm as well as funny central presence – and no one else could have done it.

Many years later I wrote some material for Harry for a television show. As he was doing a summer season at the Palladium, I visited his dressing room several times and fell chatting about various things. On one occasion we got into a discussion about the different theories of the nature of time.

Later that year we discovered we were holidaying at Christmas in the same place. When we met up there the first thing he did was to give me a copy of the book *Time* by J.B. Priestley.

Need I say more?

Kiri Te Kanawa

*'We're a Couple of Swells,' sang Harry alongside the
superb voice of Kiri Te Kanawa as they pranced around the
stage dressed as tramps on one of Harry's television shows.
He announced how proud he was to present exciting new
talent on his show, and how he predicted this bright young
singer from the Covent Garden Opera Company had a
great future ahead of her. She did, and still remembers
Harry with great fondness.*

Harry has this beautiful natural voice, which was a joy
to hear every time we worked together. He's had his up's
and downs, but God has been there for him, and Harry's
incredible faith in God has brought him through the worst
times. His strength I admire.

Bruce Forsyth

*Harry has made and kept many friends in the business,
including the original star of* Sunday Night At The
London Palladium *and* The Generation Game, *who
also has a huge number of television game show and theatre
appearances to his credit.*

Harry and I were both on the bill at Cleethorpes. Harry
was the top of the bill, and you really had to look for my
name somewhere at the bottom. Arriving at the theatre I
discovered that I was supposed to be sharing a dressing
room with six dogs from an act called 'Duncan's Collies'. I
did try, but they were all over the place and I was worried
about taking my trousers off – it was a nightmare! So there

I was, putting my tap shoes on in the corridor beside the stage door, when Harry walked in and asked what the problem was. When I explained he invited me into his number one dressing room. I said he couldn't do that because he was top of the bill, but he insisted and asked me to take whichever corner I liked.

When I became a top of the bill many years later, I tried to be like Harry. Harry the person.

Jimmy Tarbuck

Comedy host to many television specials, Jimmy made his name in both theatre and clubland as one of the best stand-up comics of his generation. He is also a golf fanatic and a lifelong friend of the Secombes.

Harry taught me so much over the years, and it's a great sadness to me that when a television audience sees him singing, they sometimes forget what a great comedian he is. He's a naturally funny guy because he's got funny bones. There are men who say funny things and there are funny men. Harry is a funny man. When he's firing on all cylinders he's a wonderful comic and very quick witted.

He was at Buckingham Palace one day when in the company of a 'Hooray Henry' who was obviously boring the Queen. 'Have you ever tried rook pie, Ma'am?', the dreary man asked.

Harry looked at him and said, 'Probably not, but have you read any good rooks recently?' The Queen roared with laughter as Harry walked away.

When I was still a young man I went into a show with him for eight weeks at the Palladium called *London Laughs*. It ran for ten and a half months, and was the most joyous time of my life – going into show business at the age of 24 and learning from such a fine, fine teacher was very special. He taught me how to be decent, how to love other human beings, how to be kind, how to be humble and how to break wind before going on stage!

I couldn't believe it when they included that last comment of mine on the recent *Songs of Praise* special tribute, but that is how Harry is, and why it was such fun to work with someone who is essentially a naughty schoolboy. It was a daily joy to to work with Harry. Once on the stage he would say the most disgracefully funny things out of the side of his mouth, and I would burst out laughing and get told off by the management.

Harry gave time. He would never be so presumptuous as to give me notes after my performance, but if I asked for advice he was always readily available to open up the 'book' and give a few hints. Even though we are two quite different comics, Harry taught me a lot about audience timing and control during that show, how to hold them, let them off the rein a bit, and then pull them in again.

Harry also realized that a little adulation is good for the soul, whilst too much is very dangerous. Too many stars surround themselves with 'yes' people who are unable to give an honest opinion. Harry was never like that. One day he took me to one side in his dressing room and said, 'You're going to be put in a very elevated position, young man. It's very nice to be big, but you don't have to be very big to be nice.' I thought that was terrific.

Creed never came into it with Harry. He loves his fellow man, and doesn't understand prejudice against colour or any other supposed obstacles. Every time he came on stage, a wave of love would flow over the footlights and into the audience.

Through being with Harry you catch a social conscience,

which makes you aware of how you can help others less well off than yourself. Harry has had this effect on me and my family time and time again. My life has been that much better for knowing Harry and Myra. They go together like roast beef and Yorkshire pudding, or eggs and bacon.

If there is going to be sainthood, this guy should get it. We all adore him, and I love him madly.

Bill Pertwee

Despite his books, his numerous radio and television roles and stage appearances, Bill will probably always be known as Warden Hodges in Dad's Army. *And as a fan of Harry's too!*

I only worked with Harry on a charity concert in Manchester some while ago, but it was enough to realize that he is indeed a national treasure. As a fan of his I can only say he radiates this feeling of warmth throughout our business and the general public.

He has conquered every medium: radio, television, films and musical theatre. What more could one ask of a performer? Harry and Myra have always been an affectionate and friendly couple, and goodness, what great ambassadors for show business!

Roger Kemp

Fellow performer Roger Kemp admires the way Harry covered any onstage faux pas with a gag.

I remember one incident in particular during rehearsals for *The Plumber's Progress*. Harry was playing the upstart new member of a small-town German quartet – with a superb tenor voice.

Falling for another member's sister to the outrage of the rest of the quartet, Harry, up a ladder propped against a bedroom window, was serenading his lady love in the moonlight – and at full volume. Coming to the end he paused, listening, waiting for her reply, or better still her appearance.

Silence within.

Turning out front and improvising to no one in particular, he murmured, 'She must be deaf.'

As far as I remember the line was kept in. Harry, throughout, was a delight to work with.

Our paths have crossed on a number of occasions. The first time I was aware of the existence of Sir Harry was actually about fifty years ago, when I saw him on TV.

Years passed by and he was starring in the musical *Pickwick* at the Saville Theatre in London. I booked a seat and looked forward to seeing him 'live' at last. Sadly the night I went he was off sick with a bug.

Some years later he and Roy Castle did *Pickwick* together especially for the BBC, and I was asked to play a minor role in it. Of course I was thrilled. The day we recorded the musical, poor Harry was suffering from a bad attack of the flu but Harry being Harry, he bravely carried on and gave a great performance alongside the wonderful Roy.

When I moved to Sutton, I discovered that Harry was already living there and found to my astonishment that he had a house right opposite the cricket ground. Now I love cricket! He played many a charity match there and I went to as many as possible. Amazingly, his performances on the pitch were as good as the ones on stage.

His work with the Taverners, a wonderful organization created to give youngsters a sporting chance in life, has been immeasurable. Harry has that rare magic, a gift that God himself has given him, and one that he has always been prepared to use for the benefit of others.

David Merrick

The producer and impresario is famous for his major stage musicals, such as 42nd Street *and* Pickwick.

He's the eighth wonder of the world.

Lord Rix

Infamous for the Whitehall farces in which he dropped his trousers each night, Lord (Brian) Rix has spent a lifetime in the entertainment business and now concentrates on raising funds for an array of charities, particularly MENCAP. Harry has done a great deal of work for charity and Lord Rix has known him quite a number of years. However, on this occasion Lord Rix probably wished he hadn't asked Harry at all!

Harry was short-sighted and so was an indeterminate batsman. At a charity match a young Freddie Trueman was bowling to Harry at half pace but then decided to throw in a fast one for a laugh – it was very, very fast and in addition it was a yorker.

Unfortunately it hit Harry on the foot and damaged it. Harry made a great performance out of this, hopping about and milking the incident for the benefit of the spectators who were laughing so much. The crowd did not realize that he was genuinely in pain and thought it was all part of the show, a great moment of acting.

Harry had to have his boot cut off.

Ruth Madoc

Well known for her appearances in the classic television series Hi-De-Hi, *Ruth is an accomplished actress and entertainer who is particularly grateful to her Welsh compatriot.*

When I was just eleven I wrote to Harry Secombe. As a budding performer I was eager to know how to get into the business and thought that Harry was the best person to contact. The principality of Wales is very proud of Harry and others like Ossie Morris and Gladys Morgan. I used to listen to Harry on the radio doing *Welsh Rarebit* every Friday night and wished I could be like him. Every time they finished the programme with him singing 'We'll Keep a Welcome in the Hillsides', I used to end up in tears with the emotion of it all. Harry was a big hero to me.

Having sent my letter and cassette to Harry, in my heart I thought I would never hear from him. I was wrong. Rather than dismiss me as a silly little child, he took me seriously and sent my tape on to his one-time manager Frank Barnard. Harry obviously knew that Frank was the best person to take care of my budding but vulnerable talent, and would look after me properly. Although Frank never became my agent, he spent a lot of time pointing me in the right direction, and it was he who eventually prepared me to audition for the Royal Academy of Dramatic Art. He introduced me to a lady called Sonny Rogers, who became the 'feed' to Frankie Howerd, and she coached me when I was just fifteen. Amazingly, I got into RADA, and I was so proud when Sonny came to see me in *42nd Street* recently. It was Harry who graciously set my career rolling, being the first link in the chain. I owe quite a lot to him, and I love him dearly.

Through the years I gradually got to know Harry as we bumped into each other socially, but it was on *Pickwick* that I was able to appreciate him properly. I stood at the side of the stage one night and thought how privileged I was to be working with this man, who at seventy-five years old was still hitting a top C. Not only is he a clever comic, a superb actor and a gracious celebrity, but he has this wonderful voice. They don't breed them like that now.

I noticed that Harry would arrive at the theatre early, and the door to his dressing room was always open. It was never used to shut people out, even when he was preparing to go on stage. He always had time for another member of the cast calling in to see him, and the tea and biscuits were on hand. Always.

When we opened the show at the Chichester Festival Theatre, it was all very proper and straight with some nice little moments of comedy. Then the show went on tour – we seemed to go everywhere – and things became slightly different. I was playing Mrs Bardell, and in the bed scene I had to try and seduce old Mr Pickwick. Harry is a very generous performer, and even said to me one night that I could lead the bed scene patter and he would follow me. Not many leading men are confident enough in themselves to let go in such a way.

So what started off quite kosher in Chichester soon became a riot of comedy once we were on the road. Harry and I ad-libbed tremendously as we threw ourselves around the huge bed. The scene became twice as long as it was originally and Sir Harry as Pickwick was just wonderful, throwing out all the funny voices as I bounced around showing my bloomers. The audience loved it and howled more and more each night. When poor Patrick Garland, our director, came to see us, he just threw his eyes heavenward, while Mr Dickens turned in his grave! I still get people coming up to me five years later to say that they remembered the bed scene and what fun it was.

Myra is an institution in her own right. The most wonderful thing about Harry and Myra is their humility. I always call them Sir Harry and Lady Secombe, and when they try and brush away my formality I complain because I love calling them that. It's so fitting for them both, and I just can't imagine one without the other. They are synonymous.

I noticed how Myra was always close by, and I've taken a few leaves out of Harry's book over the years, but the one I appreciate most is having John, my husband, around when I'm away on tour so much. John sometimes looks up at me and states in a strong Welsh accent, 'I'm another Myra!'

'Yes, you are,' I tell him. And what a compliment!

Saintly Secombe

Ten years of Highway *made a big difference to me, and firmed up my own personal faith considerably.*

HARRY SECOMBE

From his earliest days, Harry's heart was a spiritual one. His experiences as a lad in church were dull and boring, yet they sowed the seed of his love of music and reverence for God. Although it was not the usual routine for the family to pray together, Harry himself was seen and heard each night kneeling at the foot of his bed, praying with all the sweetness of Christopher Robin and all the sincerity of an archbishop. There was always a sense in which God had a guiding hand on Harry's life, and Harry was frequently aware of this, as was brother Fred.

Fred had discussed the topic of God versus the theatre on many occasions. In a little green book called *The Theatre – An Essay*, the Church of 1841 had already clearly described its thoughts on the entertainment business: 'An actor is one of the vilest vermin that hell hath ever

175

vomited out ...' was its most memorable description.

When Fred became chaplain of the Swansea Grand Theatre he had a chance to bring together these seeming opposites, and encouraged the Bishop of Swansea to attend the pantomime service he had prepared that year. In his sermon, the Bishop used a carefully chosen Bible passage that showed how God made the dolphin simply to entertain him, and how God therefore believed in the value of being entertained. Not only that, said the Bishop, but the gift of music and laughter must surely provide one of the best vehicles for preaching the Gospel. Was Jesus not a man of wedding parties and a user of comical storytelling in order to get his message across? Surely God must have had a sense of humour in making us? Fred was to continue and develop this idea in his many popular and amusing books based on the life of a clergyman in a small community.

Fred was quite happy to carry into any theatre the message that God loved the singer, dancer, juggler and comedian. Wearing his dog collar proudly past the stage door he was equally at home chatting to the many and varied performers he met along the way. He particularly enjoyed visiting his brother whenever he could. 'When I first went to see *Pickwick* in 1963, I was so convinced by Harry's character that I forgot he was my brother!' remembers Fred. 'Even though I only saw the first half.' Having gone backstage in the interval, Fred was surprised to see legendary comedian Tony Hancock sitting in the dressing room. Hancock seized the opportunity to ask a man of God his opinion of whether he was doing the right thing by joining up with comedy partner Sid Field, or whether he would do better on his own. They chatted for so long, while Harry appeared and disappeared to go on and off stage, that it was 1 a.m. before they finished. This incident, and the fact that he invited Tony back to his home in

Cheam afterwards, illustrates Harry's genuine sense of hospitality.

'Whenever I walked into a theatre,' says Fred, 'people would surround me and want to talk about God. No one ever laughed or made fun. There was a lot of respect. So when Tony Hancock wanted to talk about faith, it was no surprise to me. Sadly he was a crazy, mixed-up man who was spiritually sitting on the fence, and desperately wanted a bolt out of heaven to convince him. Of course, God doesn't work like that. If he did, there would certainly be no need for faith or trust.'

And when Harry attended the opening of Fred's new church, he was so eager to please his brother that he forgot the words of his song. Harry must have sung 'Bless this House' thousands of times, and yet the incident showed how every performance is vitally important to him, no matter how many times he has done it. As usual, while Harry got a joke out of the situation, he started again and made sure that next time he was word perfect.

'Harry has not only been a superb comic, an affectionate man, and a good brother, but a very close friend,' smiles Fred. 'He's been a great support to me, even in the most trying of times.'

While the Reverend Fred was busy taking the church into the entertainment business, Harry was taking the entertainment business into the church.

Highway was first broadcast on Remembrance Sunday in 1983, and Durham Cathedral provided the perfect backdrop for this new series which was seen as a direct threat to the BBC's long-running *Songs of Praise*. Its format, however, was somewhat different, and because it was transmitted at a slightly different time from its rival, viewers were served up a double 'God-slot' each Sunday.

Actress Wendy Craig was Harry's first special guest.

'When I first did *Highway*, Harry was extremely welcoming and invited me into his special mobile caravan. It had *Highway* written on the side in big letters and it was Harry's comfortable base while recording. The series took him to some strange and isolated places all over the country and it was important to have somewhere to rest and prepare for the shoot.

'The caravan took him everywhere and had everything on board that he needed, including beds, a kitchen, a loo and a settee for him to sit on while he went through the day's script with his musical director, Ronnie Cass. Whenever we chatted, however, it was not so much about business as about family. He would ask me how my brood was, and what they were up to. Having been godfather to my eldest son, Alastair, Harry was always interested in how his oboe playing was going, as well as enquiring after Ross, my other son, a writer. He regaled me with stories of his own children and above all Myra, and struck me as very much a family man.

'I filmed my reading outside Durham Cathedral and stood beside a most beautiful rose which had been cut from a plant in Picardy during the First World War. Somehow the Cathedral gardeners had managed to keep the rose blooming, as it has done every year since, and it is in itself an act of remembrance.

'When *Highway* went to County Durham I joined the team once again in a museum that had been constructed from an original mining village. All the houses, the streets and the shops were just as they would have been a hundred years ago, it was fascinating. As the programme was a Christmas special, I read a seasonal poem by John Betjeman while sitting in a tiny country cottage, an exact replica of how it would have been all those years ago. There were rugs made of rags and it was authentically furnished with what are now considered antiques!'

Though by now considering himself antique, Harry had been selected especially for *Highway*, and his name and that of the show were chosen together. Harry was initially nervous, however. While pleased to be asked, he wasn't sure that his type of humour would lend itself to such a programme, so Jimmy Grafton negotiated a contract for just six editions. In fact it was to run for twelve years, and became the most successful programme of its kind to appear on independent television. The show might involve travelling up to 25,000 miles a year, and the heavy schedule of interviewing people across the country about their faith, interspersed with songs set in all kinds of churches, was exhausting but immensely satisfying for Harry.

Nor did it label him as solely a religious performer. For some celebrities, worry about being open about their beliefs is based on a fear of being categorized. Will they expect me to preach at them rather than make them laugh from now on? Perhaps producers will not take me seriously any more? Fortunately for Harry, he had already established himself as a skilful performer, and therefore had nothing to lose.

In fact *Highway* took his expertise and stretched it in a way that Harry had never thought possible. Here he was not Mr Bumble, Humpty Dumpty or Pickwick, but the real Harry meeting real people. It was to move him, uplift him and reinforce his own faith.

Harry proved to be a consummate presenter, putting nervous interviewees at their ease and therefore getting the best possible interview. He was respected as a big star, and yet he was able to meet ordinary people on their own level, becoming an instant friend.

Harry recognized all this from day one and said that very soon *Highway* became a new way of life for him. Previously, when Harry had toured the provincial theatres, he had been all round Britain, but it had been a 'hit and run' situation. Arriving at the stage door directly from his digs, he would rarely come into contact with the people who lived in the towns. Harry seldom met the audience individually, except for the autograph hunters at the stage door, and left each town without getting to know anything about it or those who lived in it. Now, meeting so many ordinary folk who had done extraordinary things, he realized that there was a tremendous amount of good being done, quietly and without thought of reward, throughout the country.

Alongside his local guests, Harry invited as many of his old show-biz mates as possible to sing. The 'backstage' result was that many in the profession were given a gentle nudge to consider where they themselves stood spiritually. Harry didn't even have to open his mouth; that would anyway have been uncharacteristic.

Harry's abilities were stretched once again when after a long and successful run, *Highway* was controversially brought to a close and its format updated into a new show called *Sunday with Secombe*. This was a morning programme, but the biggest difference was that it was live. Harry's ability to keep anxious guests calm, or overcome the nightmares of machinery breaking down, while bringing such a homely feel to the programme, was crucial. While co-presenter Kaye Adams brought glamour and an important element of female interest to the programme, many believe that no one but Harry could have made it the success that it was.

Harry's ability to bring ordinary people's lives to the small screen in such a natural way, meant he was an obvious choice when the BBC's *Songs of Praise* began looking for an additional presenter. With *Highway* and *Sunday with Secombe* now replaced by an in-studio magazine programme, which many considered to be one-dimensional after Harry's generous style of presentation, the BBC was now free to snatch Harry back.

With many happy memories of 'Auntie' behind him, it was a pleasure for Harry to return to old ground. Co-presenter Pam Rhodes remembers the excitement that everybody felt when they heard he was about to join them. 'We were simply thrilled to bits when Harry came over to *Songs of Praise*. For many years *SoP* and *Highway* had enjoyed a friendly rivalry. Several times we would be filming and a helicopter would fly overhead. So we had to stop filming, and joked that it was Harry up there checking on us.

'He not only added a sense of fun, but also brought with him all the affection that the British people have for him. He added a gravitas to the programme, partly because he was always very comfortable in churches, having grown up in the choirboy tradition. He has always unashamedly loved hymns and singing, and brought his own wonderful voice with him.

'He was invaluable in marking the special occasions of the war years, the fiftieth anniversaries, and of course Remembrance Day. He added a very special dimension to that because of his own wartime experience. He understood with empathy, without the need for words. The most moving time of all was when he went with a 102-year-old veteran who had lost his best friend in France during the First World War. Harry travelled with him across to the war grave and accompanied the old soldier as he visited for the first time the place where his eighteen-year-old friend had died.

'It was so many years ago, and yet this lovely 102-year-old man wept. The image of Harry standing there beside the old man in the wheelchair as he cried was extremely touching. Harry stood there in silence, just knowing when to let pictures speak for themselves and let this old man have his private grief.

'He was such a wonderful companion for the old soldier, and yet the real story is that just before it was filmed Harry had heard that he had prostate cancer himself. He was also dealing with his own grief, bereavement and shock, as he stood by that grave.'

Not many years previously, Harry had been shocked by the diagnosis of a similar cancer in his friend and Goon colleague Michael Bentine. Michael had agreed to be interviewed on *Songs of Praise* by Harry, who was surprised that he insisted on coming out of intensive care to do the interview. Harry interviewed Bentine at home, where Michael talked eloquently about death, three of his five children having passed away before him. He spoke about his own private Gethsemane one minute and had Harry and the camera crew in tears of laughter the next. When Harry left the room for a moment after the interview, he returned to find Michael flat out asleep, having been totally drained by the interview – and this beside the memory of his best pal Roy Castle. Harry was very moved by both his friends' illnesses, and within a very short space of time, here he was dealing with it himself.

'Reflecting on these friends,' says Pam, 'Harry must have stood at the graveside with a great mess of emotion and terror going on inside him, but to hold his own feelings in as he did that day and to show such empathy with the dignified old man at the graveside was enormously moving for all of us. It illustrates the measure of the man, in that he always puts other people first. His showmanship enables him to hide his own feelings and get on with the job to be done, makes everybody around him feel special, and is a rare gift.

'I probably haven't met him as many times as some, but I do work alongside people who meet him often and they always rave about him. They love being with him and bathing themselves in his sense of fun and that infectious laugh. Harry is the consummate professional; he relaxes people, greets everybody, no matter who, remembers their names and problems, and asks after them. He is neighbourly in the best sense of the word.

'He has the knack of talking to the camera as if it is one individual person that he knows, and whose opinions matter to him. He has the ability to transcend the screen and be the friend that everybody wants him to be. In some ways he doesn't perform, he just is.

'His faith has been implicit and is something that he has grown up with. His great love of hymn singing is obvious and he talks about that often. Working on the programme certainly touched him a great deal; it does when you have people sharing very intimate and sometimes traumatic experiences with you, it is tremendously encouraging to your own faith. It's also quite humbling because you wonder, if I'd been through what that person has been through, could I be sure that my faith would be as strong? The answer is that you simply don't know. It's very encouraging seeing what faith brings to people who are facing tremendous challenges in their lives. It's affected me and without a doubt will have affected and enhanced Harry's faith too.'

Guy Bennett, the London Palladium's official chaplain for more than twenty-five years, got to know during that time many of the stars who passed through its world-famous doors, and not least Harry. 'Harry is the sort of person that when you meet him, you instantly feel you know him,' explains Guy. 'Sir Cliff Richard has a similar type of personality. They might be dashing around backstage under enormous pressure, and yet they will suddenly stop to say hello and ask how you are. It's easy to see that when you talk to Harry; he's not looking over your shoulder wondering what he has to do next, it's eyeball to eyeball. He gives you his entire attention.

'On one occasion when I visited him during the run of *Pickwick* I said that I had something important to pass on to him. He smiled and chortled in his usual way and probably wondered what I was going to say. "It sounds awfully obsequious," I stammered, "but I just want to say thank you, because all my life, you have been a huge part of the laughter in it. Out of all the performers I have met and watched, you are the one I have always known to be cheerful and encouraging. You've added so much to my life, and I'm forever grateful." With my little speech over, Harry was probably pleased that I said what I did, but I was much more pleased to have had the chance to say it to him.'

With Guy's pastoral hat on, he was able to observe Harry from an angle unseen by most. 'One of the first people I interviewed when I started working for local radio was Roy Castle. Having known Roy for a number of years, I went to his home to do the recording and I remember his exact words when I asked him about life in the business: "When I first started out, I was at the bottom of the bill while Harry was at the top. I said to myself, if ever I get to the top of the bill I want to be like Harry, because Harry cares for everyone down to the stage doorkeeper's cat." I thought this was a lovely tribute to Harry, particularly as Roy's resolve came true.'

It's obvious that Harry's own Christian faith has a huge influence on the way he conducts his life. Although as solid as a rock, it's more like an iceberg, as most of it is hidden. Yet one is aware that his relationship with God is a closely personal one. 'There is a certain evangelistic aggression that one sometimes finds in the church, but not so with Harry,' explains a show business colleague. 'His faith is a very deep part of his life, and he expresses it without forcing it down people's throats, which is why we all admire him.'

The severe case of peritonitis that Harry suffered while on tour in Barbados in 1980 caused him to rethink his own faith. Harry nearly died of a perforated colon; yet one of the surgeons had deflected Harry's thanks for saving his life with 'Don't thank me, thank Him,' and pointed heavenwards. And so Harry did. He later commented that he could never have done a programme like *Highway* without a personal faith; if he had, it would have been hypocritical.

Seeing others in critical situations also affected the way he viewed heaven, and none more so than his friend Roy Castle. 'Roy and I often talked with Harry about the things that happened in our lives and our faith,' says Fiona. 'He was always open to all we had to say, and listened intently. Harry was always keen to learn, and was very aware that Roy's faith was vitally important to him at the neediest time of his life.'

Guy Bennett had the pleasure of interviewing both Harry and Roy for his Sunday morning programme and was able to question Harry a little more deeply about his own faith. 'Having travelled to his home in Surrey to do the interview, I got back home, only to find there was nothing on the tape. I rang Harry in desperation and full of apology and he put me at ease right away. "Oh, what a shame. But don't worry, boy," he said. "Pop down next week and we'll do it all again." No panic, no groans, just support. That's Harry.

'Another time he was popping into the studio to talk about the tour of *Pickwick* that he and Roy Castle were doing. I saw the show at Chichester and mentioned that I had not been able to get hold of a copy of "If I Ruled the World", as they hadn't released the CD of the show at that point. Harry told me not to worry and said that he would sort it out. I was sure that in the middle of a national tour,

185

doing eight shows a week and probably with a dozen media interviews on top, he had better things to do with his time. I tried to assure him not to bother, but he insisted that I ring him a few days later.

'On the Sunday morning "God-slot" I presented each week, I was eager to include what I called "A Song for Sunday". It was basically a well-known current pop song with a thought for the day wrapped up in it. It's surprising how many songs can be put alongside a chat about faith, particularly those from musicals, as they often contain messages about love and faith. So having Harry's most famous song for the programme was quite important.

'A few days after seeing Harry, I rang him up, and he remembered our conversation and announced that he had the record waiting to send. I offered to drive over and pick it up, but he insisted that he would send his driver over with it. Sure enough, a few hours later, his Rolls and driver arrived with a gold-labelled version of the vinyl recording. He had obviously sent out for it especially. I treasure that record today. Typical Harry.

'I think the willingness of show business people to give of their talents so freely in interviews like that says something about them. It would be difficult to find, say, an electrician or plumber perhaps, who would work for nothing. Entertainers are very generous people.

'My work has involved me organizing a series of charity shows over the years for anything from Cancer Research to different Millennium funds. Harry is the one and only person I have never had to ask for help, because he offered it himself. "If there's anything I can do to help, you only have to ask," he said one day, quite out of the blue. Of course when you are a public face you are constantly being asked to open garden fetes and things, so it's not always wise to offer.

'One day I happened to be looking for someone to help launch an appeal for our little theatre in Oxted. Harry happily asked me to contact him a few weeks later to see if he could do it, but when I rang both his secretary and Myra they said "no". This was very out of keeping with Harry's usual attitude, and I threw a little prayer heavenwards as I knew something must be wrong. A few weeks later it was announced that he had cancer.

'When I went to visit him a little later, Myra greeted me, but warned that Harry was a little bit tired as he had travelled to Evesham the previous day to open the new wing of a hospital. Evesham was a long way from their home, and it must have been very wearing for him, I thought, as I walked into his front room to greet him. If it were me, I would have been lying down on the floor groaning and feeling sorry for myself.

'The first thing I heard as I entered was a huge guffaw of laughter, and as we sat chatting, I thought, hang on, here's a chap who has been a diabetic for years, has had a stroke, has cancer and also some other disease which I can't even pronounce, and he's got me rolling around the floor laughing. Where was the self-pity? To be able to sit there with all that and still be the cheerful Harry we all knew was simply amazing. It was obvious that his faith was the real bedrock in all that he did and suffered.'

The old adage that 'behind every strong man is a strong woman' is true in Harry and Myra's case. Some suggest that Myra has been the 'power behind the throne'. Despite being a submissive woman, in the Godliest sense, she has felt that her place is to make Harry happy, and be a support to him.

Fiona Castle comments that Myra has been a strong role model in her own life. 'Myra taught me that I could be a wife in show business and not interfere in the politics of the profession, but find real fulfilment in being at home. Even in these days of equal opportunities, it was all right to be the woman that your husband wanted to come home to. Harry appreciates this and never takes her role for granted. He knows she's a gem.'

Fiona also watched Myra during Harry's illness and notes, 'She has never stopped, never given in, she is the strongest of supports. Whenever I visit she is always running around, getting me a chair and a cup of tea and some cake. I know what it is like to be a carer, because I was one, but even if I say I don't want to come if she has to look after me, she always insists. She is a lady with a big servant heart, and totally selfless. I know she hurts like anybody else, but she is so dedicated to looking after Harry, whether at home in Surrey or gaining some much-needed rest and sunshine in their Majorcan retreat.'

Harry the comic does not like being ill. Who does? Except that for Harry it's a deeper problem. Not content to switch off and relax, his mind is quick but now his body isn't. He gets frustrated when he can't get to the charity events he so loves, can't be part of the entertainment business that he loves so much. But neither does he moan. He is careful not to be a nuisance to anybody and puts a brave face on how he sometimes really feels. 'The thing about Harry,' says Fiona Castle, 'is that he has always looked at the positives in any situation. While some people by nature see the negative, Harry always sees some good in everything.'

Harry is grateful that the stroke has affected only his left side. Although walking and using the arm and leg on this side of his body is difficult, he still attacks this like an athlete running for gold. He is determined not to give in to his condition. His mind is sharp and active, though there was one moment in hospital when this too was put into question.

Harry, having arrived at a centre that specialized in the rehabilitation of stroke victims, sat awaiting his turn alongside an old chap in a wheelchair. When the old man turned and started gabbling in double-Dutch, Harry, thinking the man was having a laugh, replied with his best Goon-like nonsense. As the two of them sat there exchanging gobbledegook, the physiotherapist arrived and exclaimed to a nurse that Harry had finally lost his marbles!

'Harry, on the other hand, has always been so outgoing, and so eager to help,' says Fiona. 'This generosity can leave him open to being taken advantage of, but I think he would rather do that than miss an opportunity to help someone less fortunate than himself.'

Harry, of course, would think nothing of the kindness he shows. He doesn't view himself as any different from the next man. It's all automatic to him, and he considers it a natural response that everybody probably has. If only we all put our faith into practice in this way.

Ann Bissett

The stage doorkeeper for one of the country's favourite seaside theatres, Ann has welcomed Harry through its famous portals on many occasions.

This is the man with the song in his heart,
This is the man who takes comedy's part,
This is a man with kindness of soul,
This is a man who accepts his role,
This is a man whom we love to applaud,
And this is a man who loves his Lord.

Dame Thora Hird

*It was in 1931 that Thora first took to the stage. Since then
she has crossed the boundaries of radio, theatre, films and
television with extraordinary aplomb.*

I think I've known Harry forever. I can't remember when
we first met but it must have been late forties, I suppose.
Anyway, I'm going to be ninety soon, so I'm allowed to
forget exactly where we met, aren't I?

More than likely it was at Broadcasting House or one
of the many sound-recording theatres. Radio was so big in
those days, it's hard to realize its importance, even though I
was going from programme to programme doing half a
dozen lines in each, and being really grateful if I was in a
series. I probably met Harry when I was doing something
like *Dick Barton, Special Agent!* You'd meet so many of the
backbone of the business in the BBC canteen. That's where
they should have placed the microphones! Anyway, I did
meet Harry and we were on first name terms from the start.

We both have daughters who we adore, so when we met
it wasn't always playing the fool, you know. We'd catch
up on family and friends, although we'd always end up
laughing. Curiously enough, for two such busy people on
such a little island it's strange that we didn't work together
until the London Palladium in 1966.

My career had been mainly in drama and my biggest
successes had been in the West End until I did a TV sitcom
with Freddie Frinton called *Meet The Wife*. It was a huge
success and Freddie and I were asked to do the London
Palladium summer show. It was twice daily and three
times on a Wednesday and Saturday. Harry and Jimmy
Tarbuck were in the show, and it was lovely to see Harry

every day and share a cuppa. On the walk down at the end of the show on the opening night, things had gone well and we were happy that we'd made it through the show all right. After our bow to the audience, Harry took me in his arms and laid me across his knee à la Valentino. It got a huge cheer and a laugh, so we kept it in for the rest of the season. It was such a fun time. England won the World Cup, and even though Freddie and I faced the daily trauma of filming a new series of *Meet The Wife* during the day, and had fast cars laid on to get us to the theatre in time for the show at night, it was a truly happy experience.

Funnily enough, Harry and I must have talked about our Christian faith because we thought that we would both be identified with 'God shows' in later years. The BBC religious department first asked me to appear on *Songs of Praise* in the late seventies. After a couple of years I began presenting *Praise Be*, a spin-off from the original which had requests for the hymns. At one point there were over six thousand letters a week coming in to the BBC addressed to me personally. Sadly I couldn't read them all, so there was an office that sorted them and only sent certain ones to me.

Obviously such a success at the BBC didn't go unnoticed and very soon 'the other side' – ITV – came up with Harry and *Highway*. I was delighted. We had the most friendly and loving rivalry, but deep down I don't think it mattered to either me or Harry who the viewers chose from week to week. The fact was that television had never had bigger audiences for religious programmes on a regular basis and, by the way, never has had since.

At the warm-ups before the hymns were recorded in various churches throughout the land, there would always be jokes to the congregation about needing to sing loud enough for Harry to hear them. I know that Harry's crew did the same sort of thing; when their filming in some beauty spot was disturbed by a loud noise, they would blame me for sabotage.

At one point, I was asked to do an appeal with Harry on one of the *Highway* shows. I did this with great pleasure. Sadly, when I asked Harry to come and appear on *Praise Be*, contracts or something daft like that wouldn't allow him to do it. We were both very sad about that. Ah well, as if it would have made any difference in the greater scheme of things!

After sixteen years *Praise Be* came off the air and *Highway* followed a season or two later. New people with new ideas came into the television religious departments, all trying to make their mark, but to my way of thinking there have never been replacements for such popular God-slots since. You see, I think people identify with folk like Harry and me, we were like their own family and were always welcomed into their homes.

Needless to say, I couldn't begin to count the number of charity lunches, dinners, openings, visits and fundraising appearances Harry and I have done over the years. The Secombes are a grand couple, and I love them both. Nowadays we're both having a bit of difficulty running the mile, but so be it, we're very blessed, with love all around us and the unique British public keeping both Harry and me in their hearts as well.

Medwyn Hughes

One of the BBC's most respected producers, Medwyn not only understands the whole business of making a television programme with someone like Harry, but he's Welsh too!

'Hello Medwyn, how are you?'

'Fine, Harry. How are you?'

'Not so good. The doctor's told me I have cancer.'

It was October 1998 and Sir Harry Secombe was in France filming an item for a programme that I was producing for Remembrance Sunday that year. I was speechless as Harry continued with the telephone conversation; he could sense that I just couldn't take in what he had said. He was now consoling me and feeling embarrassed that he had put me in such a position. But Harry's like that – always sensitive to the feelings of others.

I have worked with Harry for nearly five years. It all started when the then editor of *Songs of Praise*, Helen Alexander, asked me to look after our new presenter. I felt humble at being asked to produce a man who had done practically everything in the business.

'Call me Harry,' was one of the first things he said to me – as it was to the staff at the hospital where he was admitted following his stroke in January.

Just after last Christmas, Harry phoned me with a New Year greeting and we talked for some time about this and that. His radiotherapy was due to start at the end of January and he would be out of action for some time. It had been during a routine visit to his local GP that his suspicions were aroused. He was due for his annual flu jab and it was a classic case of going in with one thing and out with another. 'How's the water works?'

'Fine,' Harry lied.

'I'll do some tests anyway, and let you know,' said the GP.

In a couple of weeks Harry was back and was told the news he didn't want to hear. 'You've got prostate cancer.'

It took a while to sink in. Harry replied: 'Does that mean I get a refund on the flu jab?' He was still able to find a line that would take the cruelty out of the situation and put everyone at ease, including himself. Jokes and gags come easily to him; he truly is a funny man.

Our conversation continued and we got around to talking about producing a programme on his journey to what we all hoped would be remission. The conversation ended with both of us agreeing with each other that here was a programme which would live up to the Reithian ideal of broadcasting. But would anybody else agree?

They did – and we were off! Well, we thought we were. It was a Friday morning at the end of January. My telephone rang. 'Harry's had a stroke; the filming will have to be called off.' It was Myra, Harry's wife. Again, I didn't know what to say. He was due to start his radiotherapy the following Monday, which was bad enough – but now ...

I kept in touch over the next few weeks, hoping for good news about Harry's condition but fearing that this was going to be one of those great programmes that would never be made. But none of that mattered now. These things put life into perspective, don't they?

Another telephone call three weeks later, this time from Harry's agent, Tony Boyd. 'Harry wants to do a programme about the stroke; give him a ring.'

After talking to Harry, it was obvious that we had to carry on, but now with a different programme from the one we had originally planned, although as a result of the stroke the radiotherapy treatment for his prostate cancer had been put on hold.

Filming began three weeks after the stroke. On the very first day it was quite obvious that we were on to a winner and that, in a way, Harry was gaining therapeutically from the filming. He was working again.

Over the coming months, there were some very emotional moments but also some very funny ones. Harry wanted to carry on with the programme so that others could benefit from seeing his personal journey, a journey in which his faith was always present and which gave him great support during the bad times.

I wanted Sian Rees to direct the programme, but she was away filming in Israel on another of our projects. At times Sian and I have a telepathic way of working (that's my explanation for not communicating effectively). She's also a close friend of Harry and Myra's.

After our Easter broadcasts, we were both on board and the programme began to take shape. It was now scheduled as the first of the new series of *Everyman* under Ruth Pitt. Ruth liked what she had seen of the rushes and Harry was getting better. He was walking and he had some movement in his left arm. But the most incredible thing was that following only two hormone injections, his prostate cancer had miraculously disappeared.

After about eight months, Harry got a visit from one of his oldest pals, Spike Milligan. He arrived an hour early and we weren't quite ready. Harry and Spike got on like a house on fire and all the old stories came up – but were we going to miss all the best bits? We were finally ready, and what we ended up with is some of the funniest off-the-cuff television I have experienced. I think we have been able to capture some of the Goonish humour while still being focused on the theme of the programme, but I would say that, wouldn't I?

All who have worked on this programme have been touched by the wit, courage, intellect and warmth of Sir Harry Secombe.

Don Maclean MBE

A comedian holding his own private pilot's licence, Don jets with ease from summer season and cabaret to pantomime and his BBC Radio series Good Morning Sunday *in his own aircraft.*

I am a product of the Goon generation. This show was the high spot of my week and the sole topic of conversation the following day at St Philip's Grammar School. I could do all the voices and I'm sure this started me on the slippery road to performing.

I've worked several times with Sir Harry; the most memorable was a concert at the Barbican Centre in London. There was just Harry, the Band of the Women's Royal Army Corps, and me. I realized I couldn't work with a show-biz giant like him and not refer to him in my own act.

'I've not told anyone at home that I'm working with Sir Harry,' I announced to the glowing audience. 'We don't like the Welsh in Birmingham and with good reason; I'm sure they wee in our water!'

Harry opened the second half with a magnificent bit of Puccini. The audience were enthralled. He acknowledged the applause, took a drink from a glass of water on the piano, spat it out and boomed, 'Tell that Don Maclean he was right!'

A few years ago, a statue to Tony Hancock, who had been born in Birmingham, was unveiled in the city. Sir Harry, who had known Tony well, performed the ceremony. Afterwards we went to the Albany Hotel for a very posh lunch attended by numerous dignitaries. Jasper Carrott and I were each asked to make a small contribution (no more than sixty seconds) prior to lunch. The toastmaster beckoned to me and I made my way to the top table to stand directly behind the principal guest. I began,

'My lords, ladies and gentlemen and Sir Harry. No, not Sir Harry. To me he's always been Neddy Seagoon.' At which the said knight of the realm jumped to his feet, put his arm around my shoulders and squealed 'Ying tong iddle I po!' The whole crowd dissolved into laughter.

He's made life wonderful for a pro like me. There are those who think that medicine can't be any good unless it tastes awful. There are Christians who think that to be really religious you have to be boring and deadly serious. Sir Harry has proved otherwise; a life of fun and laughter can go hand in hand with a firm belief in and a love of God.

For me the measure of his comedic talents is the fact that the lovely Lady Myra still laughs at everything he says, even after fifty years.

Malcolm Flanagan CBE

Former variety director Malcolm Flanagan was responsible for numerous live television shows over many years, including Live at Her Majesty's *for LWT.*

I remember Harry's 'weight loss campaign'. He came on to a live ITV show I was directing in 1978 and suggested beforehand that, to prove his success, he would sing 'Amazing Grace' in his vest and pants, live on TV.

As it was a family show, I sought advice and permission was granted. Despite having lost many pounds in weight and size he lost no volume or tone and kept a straight face throughout.

At the finale he came on in new evening dress with the comment, 'It's cost me a fortune in new clothes since I became a new man,' patting his tummy and winking, then finishing with 'Bless this House'. Only Harry could do this – not one complaint was received.

My most recent memory of Sir Harry Secombe is from the stage show *Pickwick*. Roy Castle was appearing with Sir Harry at the Alexandra Theatre, Birmingham. Roy was unwell, but got through the performance – just!

At the curtain call, Roy walked on – he couldn't run because he was always out of breath – and received tremendous applause. As top of the bill, Sir Harry came on last, and as he passed Roy he took him by the hand and they both shared a top-billing ovation. This was not false modesty; Sir Harry knew how exhausting the show was for Roy and wanted his tremendous efforts recognized.

Neither I nor the audience knew that Sir Harry had been Roy's best man. After the audience calmed down, Sir Harry mentioned this and capped it by saying 'And we thank you – don't we, Roy?' Both nodded and walked off stage to a standing ovation.

A truly kind act by Sir Harry. Roy died of cancer only a few months later.

Dora Bryan OBE

Dora's life in film, stage and television has made her a national treasure.

I remember Harry as a lovely, warm man. A real Christian.

Steve Chalke

A founding director of the Oasis Trust, Steve has experienced both sides of life. As a television presenter he has interviewed some of the most glamorous and richest people in the country, yet with the Oasis Trust he has seen some of the worst deprivation poverty can bring. It all inspires him to move mountains in the effort to show that everybody is equal in God's eyes.

As a fellow *Songs of Praise* presenter, I am aware that Sir Harry has always been a huge hit with the audience. Whenever he presents the show, the audience figures go through the roof. In fact, in *Songs of Praise* circles, Harry is legendary. Many stories circulate about him, but my favourite is undoubtedly when Sir Harry was interviewing a decidedly stuffy bishop for the programme. Before the interview he courteously asked this rather senior cleric for clarification about how to address him. The bishop pompously replied, 'Bishop will do.' With razor-sharp wit, Harry came back with his reply: 'That's fine – and you can call me Sir!'

Wendy Craig

With shows such as Not In Front of the Children, And Mother Makes Five *and* Butterflies, *Wendy Craig has become an English television comedy institution. Her recent stage performances at Chichester and with the Royal Shakespeare Company have been focused on laughter, which she says is an essential part of both life and Harry Secombe!*

For Alistair's christening, my husband Jack and I wanted someone to be godfather who was both sincere and would bring a sense of the fun of life, someone who had a sense of humour and to whom life was a vibrant and joyous thing. We couldn't think of anyone better than Harry.

Of course Harry was perfect in the role, and we were so grateful that he had agreed. The day itself could simply be described as a gale of mirth. Giggling, interspersed with plenty of raspberries, seemed to accompany each part of the ceremony and the luncheon afterwards. We left with minds and hearts full of jokes and fun.

I realized then that we all need to laugh every bit as much as we need to cry. A laugh can change the whole colour of your day. As an actress who has done a lot of comedy, I just love that moment when afterwards you hear the audience leaving, with their voices sounding very different from when they came in. They are happily and noisily chatting away and I'm thrilled to think that they've had a good time.

Harry seems to be constantly buoyant and jolly, and I will remember him always as 'the bringer of mirth'. That's why we love him.

Nigel Goodwin

As an actor Nigel knows better than most the frustrations, hopes and dreams of a life in show business. For over thirty years, Nigel has devoted his life to encouraging and supporting professionals in the arts, media and entertainment business to take a spiritual look at their lives through his Genesis Arts Trust.

The Goons were where I cut my teenage and twenties teeth. They were an inspired team of gifted comedians and Harry Secombe was one of the very best. His Mr Pickwick on stage was impeccable and his singing of 'If I Ruled the World' powerful and memorable, but most of all, I have enjoyed the natural, easy and effective way he communicates his faith through the various programmes he has presented for religious television.

Sir Harry's dual and equal gifts of comedy and song have endeared him to millions whose sitting rooms he has entered, allowing the doorway of our hearts (not easily penetrated) to swing wide and welcome him in as a personal friend.

Canon Bill Hall

As senior chaplain for the Actors' Church Union, Bill Hall knows all about the behind-the-scenes pressure of life in show business.

As a long-term fan of *The Goon Show*, I remember my first meeting with Harry very well. This was in the 1960s, in the early years of my ministry as a theatre chaplain. Throughout that ministry, I have been privileged to know more of the man behind Neddy Seagoon, with his infectious humour and youthful exuberance for life.

While presenting ITV's *Highway*, Harry interviewed me. He put me at ease as he showed me where to stand for the cameras. I made some Goon remark, to which he responded. A few days later, he sent me several *Goon Show* tapes. That generosity and his care at the interview were matched by the professional way in which he researched the subject of the interview. He was both sensitive and probing. Some fifteen years later, at the time of the centenary celebrations of the Actors' Church Union, the same care and professional skills were still in evidence as he interviewed me for *Songs of Praise*. Again, he had carefully prepared for the interview, despite his knowledge of the ACU as its longest-serving vice-president – a fact of which the ACU is justifiably proud!

With apparent ease, he constantly moves from music to comedy and back again. This ability to combine the emotive power of music and comic inventiveness is a great gift. Through music and comedy, we can get some sort of perspective into our most passionately held beliefs and values; we may even be able to laugh at our failure and success; we can affirm life itself and we might dare to hope. That is what makes us human. That is the perspective from which we appreciate Harry's creative talent. Behind that talent is a warm and generous, much-loved man – and this, we celebrate most of all. To these qualities, we add courage, movingly apparent in the television programme featuring his response to his stroke. Here was a courageous man offering hope to others.

Picking up on the biblical theme of God at play, theologian Harvey Cox has depicted God as winking at us, 'his all-too-serious creatures'. Perhaps, with Harry in mind, he might also have depicted him blowing one of those famous Secombe raspberries!

Sir Cliff Richard

Sir Cliff, still the 'bachelor boy', remembers
Harry with great affection.

None of us finds it easy to smile, to be warm and good-humoured all of the time. Perhaps Harry doesn't either, but somehow he manages it.

At the memorable VE Day celebrations at Buckingham Palace in 1996, he was like a father figure – enthusiastic, funny, responsible, and hugely confidence-boosting. And his thoughtfulness and practical concern for our mutual friend Roy Castle in the months before his death reflected a man of deep compassion and Christian faith.

There are few stars in our industry that haven't been affected to some degree by show-biz glitz or massaged egos. Harry is the exception. With him, what you see is, happily, what you get. As you'll gather, he has my unreserved respect.

Canon Max Wigley

*Max Wigley, a theatre chaplain, holds fond memories
of Harry.*

I was in my teens and early twenties when I used to listen to *The Goon Show*. It was the ridiculousness of it all that you created in your mind as you listened to the dialogue, the combination of Harry with Spike Milligan, Peter Sellers and the rest, which made you laugh. The sound effects, Harry's laugh, Spike saying 'He's fallen in the water', all created a wonderful illusion in the mind's eye. Oh, the glory of radio!

It's difficult to put into words the 'Ying tong iddle I po' of it all, but the simple, sheer nonsense of it was wonderful. Spike telling the rest that he had a message and, when told to push it under the door, saying he couldn't. When asked why, he said it was in his head! It all sounds rather sad now but it was such wonderful, harmless fun. We have lost the ability to laugh at such things today. They would not be sophisticated enough for folks today. Or would they?

Kaye Adams

Television personality Kaye was Harry's long-suffering co-presenter on Sunday with Secombe. *No matter how serious the topic, a raspberry was always at hand!*

There will be no end of people who have funny stories involving Harry Secombe because he's a man who carries laughter around with him in the most effortless way. His humour is innate, never forced or overbearing. But for me, his greatest talents are his warmth, his generosity and his humility.

When I found out I was to be his sidekick on the ITV series *Secombe on Sunday*, I was more than a bit nervous. I'd met my fair share of 'legends in their own lunchtimes' but never the genuine article, like Sir Harry. Yet, two minutes after meeting him for the first time in a greasy spoon somewhere in South Wales, he'd blown out my apprehension with a raspberry and his trademark chuckle.

We travelled round the country every weekend for thirteen weeks and got in and out of numerous scrapes which come with live television, including having to fill for a full three minutes and ending up blathering about the weather with me convinced that Harry was going to let go a raspberry and a 'hay-ey'. Wish he had.

But the occasion which will always stick with me was at Great Ormond Street Hospital in London when Harry sang 'Somewhere Over the Rainbow'. I'm not sentimental but that left me with a tear in my eye and a lump in my throat.

Rev. Richard Dormandy

This Reverend is renowned for wearing bright red glasses and mauve Dr Martens when he preaches, not to mention the electric guitar hung and played over his cassock.

How can I forget Harry's infectious giggles, coupled with the earnest way in which he would sing – from operatic aria to Welsh song and hymn? As a boy, I could never understand the attraction of someone who could be so silly one minute and so serious the next – but then that's variety, isn't it! Of course I can understand it now – though I still warm to the 'silly Harry' more than the 'serious singer Harry'. I can only admire someone who could make the move to religious broadcasting and do it so successfully without fear of being labelled.

John Forrest

John Forrest is the creative inspiration behind many of the BBC's most original Sunday programmes. Having produced Songs of Praise at the Pantomime *and* West End Praise *from London's Victoria Palace, he has also been the force behind many other innovative programmes, including the world's largest choir of over 40,000 at Old Trafford football stadium.*

I have only worked with Harry once. This was making a programme about golden weddings. It was a delight how he and Lady Myra were so enthusiastic about taking part, and how they were more than happy to let us film them remaking their marriage vows in front of the cameras. It was a testimony, I think, not just to what great people they both are, but also to how special their own relationship is.

Vince Hill

Although he can probably chant 'Edelweiss' in his sleep, Vince loves any opportunity to sing, and is still the number one crooner we love to hear during his theatre tours and cruises.

Being invited to appear with Harry on *Highway* was more of a privilege than a job. In fact Harry's personality that day was so large that everything else about the recording has been erased from my mind. Where it was, whether it was outside or inside, what the weather was like or if the song I sang went smoothly or not have all been over-whelmed by Harry's just being there.

I do remember the song, though, it was 'Pray for a Laugh', the intermezzo from *Cavalleria Rusticana*, and I could have sworn Harry was humming along with me, such was his concern to support my labours. Perhaps it was recorded in a field in front of a castle somewhere, but I know the title 'Pray for a Laugh' struck a chord with Harry.

Working with Harry supports what I have often said about our business, that the bigger the star the nicer the person, and the easier they are to get on with. Harry certainly doesn't have to prove anything, and I found him to be an absolute delight.

I have been a fan of the Goons for a long time and love those strange words that Harry comes out with: 'Sapristi Ruckus!', 'Baddle-biddle-burp-ah!', 'Smails of loon!' and all the others which are impossible to pronounce, impossible to spell, and yet somehow inside, you know what they mean!

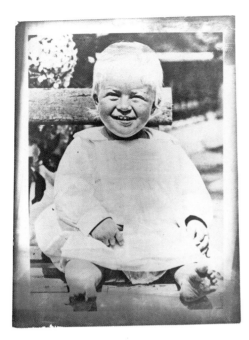

He was probably laughing even
before he was born – Harry as a
one-year-old. *Aquarius Library*

'Ready for inspection, Sir!'
Harry, on the left, with his
brother Fred. *Aquarius
Library*

Goon for lunch? An early 1950s publicity
shot. *Photograph by Harry Goodwin*

'Come in, the door's open!' Harry relaxing off-stage in 1955. *Hulton Getty*

'It went thataway!' Harry with fellow Goons Spike Milligan, Peter Sellers and the Prince of Wales. *Personal Collection*

Harry, Michael, Spike and Peter devouring another Goon script in 1951. *Hulton Getty*

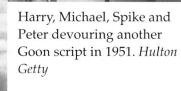

Left holding the baby. Harry is godfather to actress Wendy Craig's son Alastair. *Hulton Getty*

The Secombe Saga, with choreographer Paddy Stone and Leigh Madison. *Hulton Getty*

Take 41! Harry is caught in the clappers at Elstree film studios during the making of *Davy* in 1957. *Hulton Getty*

'You sing it and I'll try and play it!' Harry at the piano with Myra, Jennifer and Andrew. *Atlantic Syndication*

Humpty Dumpty, with Sally Smith as Mary, Mary, Quite Contrary. *Central Press Photos*

The Rolls Royce of engines and entertainers in 1961. *Atlantic Syndication*

Not even a smile for Secombe – with Roy Castle, Myra and Rev. Fred Secombe at David's christening in 1962. *PA News*

Smiles all round – receiving his OBE at Buckingham Palace in 1963. Myra, Jennifer and Andrew were on hand to make sure Harry didn't lose it! *Atlantic Syndication*

A final addition before Jimmy Tarbuck and Harry open in *London Laughs* at the London Palladium in 1966. *PA News*

Stick for sale? *Oliver!* with Mark Lester. *Rex Features*

'I said bite the bullet!' – Harry rehearsing for *The Four Musketeers*, at the Theatre Royal in Drury Lane, 1967. *Hulton Getty*

In training again – Harry limbers up with Sergeant instructor Norman Millar and Company Sergeant Major instructor Ray Emery for *The Four Musketeers*. *Army Benevolent Fund*

I love the skill of the comedy, and perhaps would have ventured into the art myself except for the fact that I can't remember the gags! Isn't it strange that I can hold a thousand song lyrics in my head but can't remember the tag line of a joke! Of course Harry is the opposite; he is the great gagger, yet is fearful of forgetting the lines of his songs. Thank goodness we're all different.

Fortunately music and laughter go well together, with music providing the emotions and laughter being the lifeblood. Laughter is an important element in my own shows to link my songs, and invites a spontaneous response from an audience, but I could never do it like Harry. He is able to provoke instant laughter, often without even having to open his mouth. Tommy Cooper was the same. They are of a breed that if you met them in the street being really serious, you'd still laugh. Harry walks on stage and everybody smiles. It's like the sun coming out in the auditorium and has a remarkable effect on an audience.

Of all the theatres in the country that I work in, it is when I stand on the stage at the Secombe Theatre in Sutton that I remember with gratitude all that he has done. Harry's been here, Harry opened this, I reflect to myself as I wait backstage. It's one of the sad things about the business that you don't always get to work with the people you would most like to. I only worked with Harry on a few occasions, but I wish I had had the good fortune for it to be more.

In all the years of being in show-biz, and in a profession often known for its gossip and jealousy, I have never, ever heard anyone say a bad word about him. What a performance!

Noël Tredinnick

*Principal conductor and musical arranger for the
All Soul's Orchestra, Noël has been seen on numerous
occasions sporting his white jacket on* Songs
of Praise.

'No, I've Never Met A Fella Like You, Sir Harry' is a
favourite line of mine adapted, with affection, from an
original lyric from *Pickwick*. Harry Secombe has a truly rare
and outstanding comic-acting ability for such a fine, world-
class operatic tenor!

It was actually his remarkable and powerful singing
voice that first hooked me as a young, impressionable
twelve-year-old when I was taken to see the original production of *Pickwick* at the old Saville Theatre (now the ABC
cinema) in Shaftesbury Avenue. I saw the show several
times after that, with Harry always excelling so naturally
in the title role. I saved up my pocket money to collect the
cast album, and the hit 45 single of 'If I Ruled the World',
just to hear him singing so beautifully time after time after
time. 'Look into Your Heart' and 'Turkey's Bigger Than
I Earn' were two other hit songs in the show, and soon
became firm favourites. I think I'm still word-perfect on all
those numbers, having heard them so often in my teens.

Although the press weren't quite so kind to it, I personally adored Harry's next West End show, which utilized the
vast expanses of Drury Lane's massive stage. This British
musical was a comic but moving production entitled *The
Four Musketeers*. Guess who was the fourth! Again Harry's
soaring tenor voice lit up the theatre every night, as did his
lightning humour and vitality. 'What love can do…' it had
certainly '…gone and done for me' once again.

As I was such a fan of Harry from my early days, it has been an immense pleasure and privilege to work professionally with him on a number of occasions later in life. The various BBC TV *Songs of Praise* programmes where we met when I was conducting the music have always been more than a joy – and how I've thrilled to his singing at close quarters! The Bournemouth programmes with the Bournemouth Sinfonietta, the 'theatre special' from the Theatre Royal, Haymarket and, then recently, the welcome tribute edition filmed at his local Yvonne Arnaud Theatre in Guildford all stand out in my memory for Harry's gentle sincerity, his marvellous memory for old faces and, of course, the skill and beauty of his performances which are always truly masterful and wonderfully unique. 'Every head would be held up high, there'd be sunshine in everyone's sky...'

Harry Secombe has permanently deposited a lifetime's sunshine in my heart – and I am eternally thankful to Almighty God that Harry has been one *great* big beacon for me.

Secombe on Secombe

'It's very important to believe in something,' says Harry. 'If you don't know where you come from, how do you know where you are going? I've always had a fairly strong faith from a child onwards, and there are no atheists in the trenches! There one's prayers are going up all the time. Having been involved in three invasions encourages you to pray quite a bit!' he chuckles.

'I've been through a few traumas in my time, but always felt that I was being "held up" by somebody beyond myself. You don't have to go to church to pray, that's for sure. When I was on tour in Australia in 1980 I suffered a perforated colon. On the way back to Barbados to meet Myra and the kids for Christmas the abscess burst and I was in terrible pain. I didn't want to get off the plane because I was anxious to get to Myra rather than be stranded in some strange foreign hospital in the middle of nowhere. By the time I got there, I was in a fair old state, and the surgeon told Myra that I only had a fifty-fifty chance of surviving.

'As I lay in my hospital bed after the operation, I looked at my arm with all the tubes coming out of it and thought, "That's an old man's arm!" It made me relax and reassess my life.

'When *Highway* came along, I wasn't sure whether I was really the right man for the job. Did they really want a raspberry blower?! Bill Ward convinced me to have a go with six, so I agreed, and it became a way of life for me.

'Arriving at a town as an act, you don't see the people. You collect your letters from the theatre, have a cup of tea and a chat with the lads there, go into the dressing room for a kip and do the show. On *Highway* I had time to see the town and meet the people who lived there. People who had thought a lot about others and given of themselves without thought of reward. Ordinary people doing extraordinary things, not doing good deeds with an ear-splitting stealth as we sometimes do in our business. I became less cocky after that, and more thoughtful about other people and what other people did, and how they worked for each other. The series turned the spotlight on thousands of unsung saints within the community, and when I saw the strength of their faith it strengthened mine. I thought that if we all followed the Christian ethic of "do as you would be done by" the world would be a truly amazing place.

'Like the experiences of Cantor Ernest Levy of Glasgow, who had been in eleven different concentration camps in Germany during the war and yet felt no bitterness for those who had treated him so harshly. As he told his story, simply and with no histrionics, all of those involved in the recording were in tears. There was a shining sincerity in the man that transcended all the evil that had been done to him, adding a new dimension to what tolerance and forgiveness really mean. When you meet people who have been through monstrous experiences like that and still you see that their faith shines through, it can be quite challenging to your own convictions.

'Strangely, the most difficult ones to interview on the show were the clerics. I suppose they were so used to appearing in a pulpit that it was sometimes difficult to break them down into being normal and natural. I used to have a chat with them before we faced the cameras, perhaps asking them what they had had for breakfast to help them relax. Plundering my mind for a question during one difficult interview with an archbishop, I asked what the highlight of his first year in office was. He said it was a fire in the roof. I was so stunned at his solemn reply that I was lost for words.

'I'm a great believer in having a rock-solid, basic faith, rather than a "frothy" one. I get upset when the so-called intellectual clergy knock away the props of the faith. When that bishop started questioning the reality of the virgin birth and the resurrection, it wasn't helpful, and threatened to destroy people's faith. Fortunately God is stronger than all that.

'It's been a privilege going around the country and visiting plenty of churches and clergy. Some are fine and some aren't. To some it's just a job, to others it's a sincere belief, and is seen as such in the way they conduct their own lives. Most of all, it's so obvious when a church is working together.

'On television and in the theatre things only really work well when people are functioning together. Not individual stars, but in programmes like *Dad's Army* where everybody is working together, and no one is the star. Shows like *Pickwick* and *The Plumber's Progress* are my favourites because they were team efforts.

'When you're out there doing stand-up, all the pressure is on you. In an ensemble everybody shares it and so makes it more comfortable for everybody concerned. I do believe this is true, from the person who sells the tickets or the ice cream to the top of the bill. Everybody is an important team member. So it is in real life, because if you all pull together the end result is terrific.'

There is no better example in Harry's career of this type of teamwork than that of the Goons, who not only live in history but remain in the mind today. 'The Goons are always funny, probably because the shows were never topical. Nothing dates a comedy show more than contemporary references. We spent most of the time rolling around the floor in hysterics.

'It was a very memorable time together at a period when the war had produced a lot of comics. Soldiers, sailors and airmen had developed performing skills while supplying their own entertainment in the field of war. All these young ex-servicemen were like a huge pond full of tadpoles, all swimming around. Some became newts, some became frogs, and others were swallowed up by the pikes. Usually called agents!

'The chemistry between the four of us was crucial, but so was the scripting from the ingenious mind of Spike, encouraged by the schoolboy humour of Sellers and Bentine. Michael was a wonderful guy in many ways and could do all sorts of things. An expert with a pistol, he could also fence well, and draw superbly. He would start with a horse's hoof and from there do the whole horse. He was a great draughtsman and a good writer. Thankfully he never took up golf!'

Harry has set examples of motivating this teamwork that many will always be grateful for. The sense of pulling together to achieve an aim seems to be at the heart of his home life too, for he and Myra have worked together as a partnership for more than fifty years. So what is the secret of their happiness?

'We laugh a lot, that's what it's all about,' he beams. 'We have a good old laugh at everything and anything, and it always keeps your spirits up. They make divorce too easy and too quick these days. There's also too much pressure on couples. I remember Stanley Baker telling me that his uncle had come to stay with him after he had been married for six months, and asked with a grin if they were on farting terms yet! Marriage is all about being real with each other, and accepting the bad as well as the good. Myra has been a most wonderful support to me, particularly on those occasions when she was able to let me go on tour or abroad and she was left looking after the kids. When the kids had grown up, it was wonderful to be able to take her with me, and I still have a picture of her standing in the wings with a glass of water and a towel saying "Come on Harry!" I wouldn't have wanted to be with anyone else. I owe it all to Myra. If it was a lottery, I got a winning ticket!!'

Harry Secombe talks with much affection about his memories from *Pickwick*. 'I was thrilled because my old mate Roy Castle played Sam Weller, although originally that part was played by Teddy Green,' Harry explains. 'Davy Jones from the Monkees pop band had been playing in the musical *Oliver!* and was asked by producer Bernard Delfont to stay on and play Sam Weller on tour. Davy was super but played it with a touch of a Mancunian accent.

'Bernie was a good man with a love of the theatre, but he was also an acute businessman. The show had made a lot of money on its American tour, and Bernie made sure that he came out personally to make sure everything was running, as it should. The show was his "baby" and he was keen to "father" it properly. On the night before we opened on Broadway, he took me out to dinner in New York and I sensed he had something on his mind. He knew that the show wouldn't quite work on Broadway and suggested that while we had had some great notices from the out-of-town critics, I shouldn't hold my breath. He was absolutely right, and before long I had caught a bad bout of mumps that put me in bed for a while. Nobody has ever replaced Bernie.

'Having Roy with me on Broadway was just fantastic. They really loved him because they appreciate the diversity of talent over there. In Britain they want to put you in a box as a singer, a comic or a speciality act, and Roy was all of these. Thirty years later when Leslie Bricusse rang me and asked whether I would like to revive *Pickwick* again, I immediately thought of Roy's involvement. His cancer was in remission then, and I thought it would be a great show to be in and revive his spirits. Of course it was his last show.

'Roy's funeral was amazing. I sat holding Fiona's hand, but it was more of a celebration time than mourning. With a jazz band playing in which most of Roy's kids were involved, it reminded me of how many different instruments he played. In my little speech I said that Roy could do anything, he could have picked up embroidery and been a master at it! It was a very lively event, Roy was a great man, and sadly there aren't many of that calibre in the business.

'I still feel him around me, particularly when I'm about to go on stage. That was the time that he and I used to have a little banter before I made my first entrance. Even now I feel him there before a performance, and the sense of his presence brings a settling kind of feeling within me.'

So what stops Harry from being caught up in all the seductive glitz and glamour of show business, becoming an egotist, and swimming in his own enormous success?

'That's a load of old codswallop, that is,' he frowns. 'I think it's been easier for me to keep my feet on the ground because of being a soldier. That makes a difference. Peter Sellers, my partner in the Goons, was a great actor, but he became cocooned against reality, and lost it for a while. He did some very daft films until the *Panther* films came along. You can't be a bastard to people and expect the best out of them.

'I have learned the secret is to respect people, and if you are in a long run, you spend more time with the cast than with your own family. Surely you want that time to be as happy as possible.' Michael Ogan, who played Willy Wardle in *Pickwick*, and Harry deliberately didn't say hello before the show so that they could make that wonderful and genuine greeting on stage each night. There was an authentic feeling of affection with everyone on stage.

'If you have a bit of a beef with someone else it's normally down to fear on their part. If you give them a chance to talk it through, it usually sorts things out pretty quickly. At the same time, of course, you can't mollycoddle other performers, you have to let them get out there and learn it for themselves.

'I've got two actors in the family, Katy and Andy. Katy is a National Theatre player and has proven herself in some wonderfully challenging roles, and Andy has done a whole series of shows, from the original *Joseph and the Amazing Technicolor Dreamcoat* in the West End with Paul Jones, to several television shows. Jennifer works at the BBC, and David. I'm very proud of them all, but I remind them not to let the starriness of the profession run away with them. Just before Katy went on in *Guys and Dolls* one day I said, "Don't forget that even though there are a thousand people all waiting for you out there, there are also two hundred million Chinese who neither know nor care that you've arrived on stage tonight!"'

Keeping things in perspective seems to be a Secombe talent, even having been in one of the world's most famous radio series of all time. Harry is understandably proud of *The Goon Show*. 'Having met Milligan in the war when he dropped this gun on me in North Africa, it's amazing how our relationship, along with the others, developed into the Goons. They were happy days, but it's been good that we've all enjoyed careers outside of that role. It's so important to enjoy what you are doing, I think either you get pleasure from doing something or you get out of it. There seem to be a lot of unhappy actors around who don't seem to enjoy what they are doing. They should certainly consider another occupation, particularly when there doesn't seem to be a lot of work about.

'Comedy is hugely important to me, and I believe it is a gift of God, but I don't think he intended us to use four-letter words all the time. This always embarrasses me when I'm watching with other people. Comedy should be able to work without adding shock value, or having to constantly use the F-word. In *The Goon Show* we used the rapier, not the bludgeon. The pay-off often used vulgar army gags, but we never felt we crossed the line. There is a sort of purity in the best forms of comedy; I despair at some of the other forms, they seem to have become twisted.

'One of my favourite poems is about a blind beggar who commentates on a show:

> No peace for those who step
> Beyond the blindness of the pen,
> To where the skies unfold.
> For them the spinning mob,
> The cross, the bow gone mad,
> The stranger on his horns.

'I find some of today's comedy very cruel. There is always a difference between laughing at somebody and laughing with them. It still seems there is a hunger for the so-called "old style" of comedy. You only have to look at the success of a programme like *Dad's Army* that millions still watch thirty years later. That's my favourite programme. We still laugh at Morecambe and Wise too, yet sadly these masters of comedy are not being replaced. David Jason is my comic hero, because he's achieved a lot in moving from comedy to the opposite role as Frost. Ronnie Barker is similar; they have such a depth of character. My favourite actor has to be Sir Anthony Hopkins, and not just because he's Welsh!

'Now that I'm incapacitated, one of the things I love to do is watch blossoming comic talent on the box, guessing who will get on and who won't make it. I'm mostly wrong, but it's fun. Of course comics these days don't have the opportunities to hone and refine their acts in the same way that we did. They practise in their parlours, rather than being able to spend a whole year visiting the venues in London, doing the same act and not having to play the same venue twice, as I was able to. By the time I had done that, the shaving sketch was as perfect as I could have made it. I was fired in the crucible of provincial variety with its non-stop shows and it was the best training ground I could have had. I brought up my first two kids on the shaving act alone.

'Then it was two shows a night at the Palladium and three on a Saturday for months. Rather than bringing stagnation, the repetition engendered perfect timing. Everybody was doing the same thing and either you learned or you didn't.

'There were no hard and fast rules about working your act in variety, apart from being at the theatre half an hour before curtain up. There was no one to advise you or direct you. It was make or break in front of an audience, and so I quickly learnt what worked and what didn't. I also learnt that as you got towards the end of the week the laughs came easier as the working week drew towards its end. Friday, which was payday, was the best night of all.

'You never went sick, because you needed the money, but today, sadly, it doesn't seem that the discipline is there among most of the young comics, and so anything goes. I wish they could have the experiences that I had. There is a certain control about the art of comedy, and I suppose it came easier to me because of the discipline I was used to in the army.

'It was very sad that we had the last reunion of my old regiment only recently. There are only seven of us left now and we're all getting on, so it was a good time to stop. Some are older than me, but I was glad that I could make it.'

Another reunion Harry recently attended was that celebrating one of the country's longest-running shows. As the special guest on the BBC's *This is Your Life* presentation, *The Night of a Thousand Lives*, Harry walked on to a standing ovation, and, remembering his first appearance on the show in 1958, said, 'I was going on holiday the following day with Eric Sykes, and the last person on earth I expected to meet was Eamonn Andrews.'

Thirty years later Michael Aspel caught him again with the big red book, during a book signing session. 'I'm delighted to be part of the show and I still watch it. There's always that element of surprise that makes it special, particularly when you start coming towards a fellow, wheeling a pram! My favourite programmes are the ones that pay tribute to the unsung heroes. Those are the ones I like best of all. I think it's a great show. Long may it continue, and God bless all who sail in her!'

So what was the most frightening time in Sir Harry's career? 'I would pick the opening of *Pickwick* on Broadway,' he reflects. 'That's because it seems that the audience is out there looking at each other rather than at you. "What's she got on tonight?" seemed more important than what was going on onstage. It's very sad really, because you have to spend more energy winning them over than concentrating on the actual performance. It was a bit like doing variety in the old days as the comic on the second spot. On you went, straight after the dancing girls, with just six minutes to get the audience on your side. We didn't have the luxury of ten or twelve minutes, so you had to grab 'em while you could.

'All that was hard work, particularly if you saw the theatre manager standing at the back of the auditorium watching intently. The fear was always whether you would get paid off and be out of a job if you didn't win them over in those first few moments. I was basically a shy person, and found that if I took my glasses off I couldn't see the audience, so I could imagine they were laughing even if they weren't. That helped a great deal in the early days!

'There were a lot of short-sighted comedians like me. Max Bygraves, Michael Bentine and Tony Hancock were three of them. Hancock was driving to do his television show one day when he had an accident and suffered whiplash. Feeling dizzy when he eventually arrived in the studio, they wrote his lines out on a card and stuck it just beside the camera. He loved it, and from then on that card was always there. When you watch the reruns of his shows, you can see him looking to the side, just off-camera.

'It wasn't until *Pickwick*, when I had to wear some Dickensian glasses with the lenses in so I wouldn't break my neck tripping over the sets, that I suddenly realized that people were taking no notice at all! In fact I saw two Japanese people fast asleep in the front row one evening.

'When I became better known it was still hard work, but in a different way. When I made my entrance they would applaud because they knew me, and now I had expectations to live up to at each performance, no matter how I was feeling at the time. They wanted and expected the best I could give, and I felt it was important to give it.

'Although I never feel sick before performances like some do, I'm still very nervous, even after all these years. I tend to walk up and down, up and down, wearing the carpet out. Often that's the time that I have prayed a lot, just before I have to go on. That's the worst moment, and our business is such a powerless one that I needed that strength to keep me going. Once I'm on, though, it's a different matter. Then I'm in charge and I'm fired up. Of course if you do develop over-confidence, it's soon knocked out of you when you get out there. You always have to work hard for laughs. If you don't, it's probably because your flies are undone! There's a basic insecurity in all comics, because you can't frame a round of applause and you can't put a standing ovation on a mantelpiece.

'Just as important to me is to stop in the wings on the way off and thank God for his help in answering my prayer. How many times have we looked back on our lives and noticed that his hand was around? We should never take things for granted, it's always essential to remember to say thank you even when things have gone wrong.'

Harry has a reputation for encouraging some things to 'go wrong' on stage himself, as many will testify. 'Funnily enough, it was when things went wrong on stage that I enjoyed it most,' confesses Harry. 'On one occasion we were at the Palladium with *Humpty Dumpty* and the safety curtain came down and got stuck three-quarters of the way down. We couldn't carry on with the show, but we made a huge joke out of it, and I ended up crawling under the safety curtain to do some stand-up patter for the audience, half-dressed as an egg!

'I can't believe that the first show I did at the Palladium was forty-four years ago in 1956! A few weeks before rehearsals began for this big event I went to New York to do the *Ed Sullivan Show*. On the way back, Myra and I stopped off at Bermuda for a short holiday and went fishing with an American friend. Carrying an American rod and American non-slip shoes, I slipped on a rock and broke my arm. Leslie Grade, the producer at the Palladium, was horrified when I telephoned him, and couldn't believe that his bill-topper was in danger of not being able to do the show. I insisted that with the help of a strong plaster on my left arm, I would be fine. I went out on stage that first night and announced to the audience, "Well, it's always been my ambition to play the Palladium with a huge supporting cast, and here it is!" It was one of the best openings I've ever done.'

The critics enthused over the show and Harry was to star again at the Palladium more times than he now cares to remember. Critics are not always kind, however, but Harry just shrugs his shoulders and says, 'Well, you just have to learn to live with it, don't you? I never like reading the bad reviews, but I think it's important, even when it hurts. On my first big film, *Davy*, a film critic said that I "sang like Caruso. Robinson Caruso!" Another one said that I should take a razor blade and cut my throat with it. It's no use letting them get you down, you must just carry on. Whatever they say, you can always learn something, and some of my worst experiences I used as material for my novel *Twice Brightly*. So something good always comes out in the end.'

Similarly, Harry's stroke was conquered through being optimistic, even though for a comedian and singer it's probably the worst of traumas to face. 'When I was diagnosed as having prostate cancer, it was a bit of a shock, but Myra and I decided we would get through it together. That would be our strength. I was marked out for a course of radiotherapy but three days before I was due to have it, I got the stroke. I went to the toilet in the middle of the night and collapsed. Myra heard and came rushing in and I lay on the floor looking at her. "Stroke," I managed to say. I knew exactly what it was.

'We were very sanguine about the whole thing, but we've always believed we should face any problems head on. While the paramedics arrived to wheel me off, Myra packed my suitcase as if I was going on holiday. There were no tears, but she held my hand all the way to Guildford Hospital where I stayed for some time.

'Myra went back home but returned every day for two months at nine o'clock to see me. As soon as I was well enough to be transferred into a wheelchair, the doctors were anxious to get me to do things. It wasn't long before I was walking with the help of crutches, and decided that I should set myself a goal. I wanted to be well enough to go to my home in Majorca by that September, six months away.

'The cancer specialist said that I was too weak to have the radiotherapy so I was given hormone injections instead every three months. When they brought the first PSA that showed how progressive the cancer was it measured 128 on the scale. After the hormone injections and a few prayers, it went down to 0.7. It's under control now, which is wonderful.

'It was just two weeks after my stroke that Medwyn Hughes, an old producer friend from the BBC's *Songs of Praise* series, arrived at my bedside. "Now it's time to do a fly-on-the-wall documentary about your stroke," he proudly announced. "It will be useful for other people to see how you are coping." I agreed and it went out as part of the *Everyman* series under the title of "The Trouble with Harry". It got five million viewers at half past ten at night, which isn't bad, is it? People in white coats talking about strokes don't really mean a thing, so I was glad to explain what was happening. I had lots of letters afterwards from people suffering similar problems thanking me for being so honest and open, so I'm really glad I did it. I'm glad it helped others come to terms with their own illness.

'I got through the frustration of not being able to move my left side very much, by thinking positively. I do get tired and a bit confused, as if the brain is having a blackout. "It's all in the mind, you know!" I still joke to myself.

'Apparently if you get a stroke on the left side of your brain, you lose the use of your right side, and more importantly, the loss of your memory and your speech. I've met a few people like that where I go for physiotherapy. They know what they want to say but are unable to speak.

'I was worried that I had lost my mind too, so it was wonderful when Ronnie Cass wrote to me and asked for a few funny limericks to go into a book he was preparing. I sent him a few and he replied by saying that they were far too sophisticated for him, and that I should publish them myself. My publishers agreed and my great mate Bill Tidy did the cartoons. We called it *Harry Secombe's Zoo Loo Book*. One of my favourites is:

> *An agnostic hyena called Tim*
> *Was always exceedingly grim.*
> *When asked, "Where's your smiles?"*
> *He said, "I've got piles –*
> *If you want me to laugh sing a hymn."*

'Another that makes me smile is:

A disgruntled old tomcat named Vince
When hearing the word "nuts" he would wince,
For his own were cut off
When they asked him to cough,
And he hasn't caught sight of them since.'

Still willing to joke about any aspect of his disability, Harry recognizes that he can't sing any more, and suggests that the nation cries 'Hurray!' So then, is it the laughter or the applause that is most important to Harry? 'It has to be the laughter, because it's the greatest response you can get. Mind you, you have to be careful, as it's possible to laugh an audience dry. If you make them laugh too much at the beginning of a show, they don't laugh so much near the end and you can find yourself exiting with a titter. That's why I used to finish with a song.'

'Falling in Love with Love' in E flat and finishing on a top D was a good exit for Harry. 'People used to like my voice and ask me to sing some more to the point at which I got embarrassed. I knew my voice was unfocused because I would sing in the wrong key and hit bum notes. So I started the singing lessons with Manilo – not Barry Manilo, but di Veroli.

'It worked, and I still have the red music books in which members of the orchestra would write pencilled notes for the benefit of the next set of musicians using them. On my band parts would be instructions like "You're OK for a pint here!" and "This break is long enough for a trip to the loo." Sometimes, if they knew the next person to be playing the part, they might leave personal notes like "How's the missus, Bert?" Our backstage equivalent is leaving a message on the dressing-room mirror in lipstick, for the next person to use your dressing room. I've left a few raspberries on them in my time.'

Imagining Harry singing 'I've had plenty of Sutton, and Sutton's had plenty of me!' He sings while he describes his time in Cheam as thirty-two years in the perfect family home. When the children grew up and left home, Harry and Myra had to find a more suitable place to live. They found it in Surrey, near Guildford. 'I've always liked the Surrey countryside, and the view across from the Weald of Sussex to the South Downs from our lounge window is inspirational to me each morning.

'I'm still surrounded by my family too. I've five grand-children now. Matthew is the eldest and belongs to my eldest son, Andrew. Andy is married to Caroline Bliss, the actress who appeared as Miss Moneypenny in some of the James Bond films. Jennifer has three teenagers, Sam, Harriet and Emily, while my youngest son, David, has a little girl called Flo. She's quite a character and will probably end up in the business too! Katy is at present unmarried and work-ing hard. I see Jennifer and Katy every week because they live quite near us, and the boys are not too far away either. We see them all at weekends when they come for Myra's grub and bring their laundry!'

If there were any regrets of not doing something in a life which has spanned every conceivable area of the media, it would have been to develop his passion for singing into opera. 'I would love to have done an opera. I chatted to Jeremy Isaacs a few months ago and was taken aback when he said that a lot of the young lads at the Royal Opera House would love to be able to sing like me!

'I think all Welshmen are natural singers. It must be something to do with the mountain air, a bit like the Swiss who yodel! The whole family would do a piece when we got together, but I was too shy. So I used to go into the out-side loo and sit there with the door open singing hymns, while the rest of the family crowded in the kitchen to listen.

It was ridiculous when you think about it, 'cos it was very cold. All the neighbours must have said "Oh no! It's that Secombe boy again, there's something wrong with him!"

'I was amazed when people wanted to take my voice seriously, because I had often played the singing side down. I always felt a bit embarrassed at the end of a Palladium show when I came out in my "singing suit". It was uncomfortable because the audience didn't know me as a singer, only a comedian. *Pickwick* changed that for me, because it helped me to be known as a singer. It wasn't a problem from then on.'

Highway was another opportunity for Harry to exercise his lungs in a good song. 'I loved the hymns because not only did they have good tunes, but the lyrics actually meant something. I was singing about something that I passionately believed in, something that I could see was changing lives.

'I still wake up in the morning with a hymn in my head. Every morning I've got a different hymn I'm singing to myself. Perhaps I should do "Fight the Good Fight" while I'm shaving? No, perhaps that would be too dangerous! One of my favourite hymns is "How sweet the name of Jesus sounds in a believer's ear", and I hum that to myself more than any other these days.

'As I look to the future, one of the poems that I find most comforting is:

> *Soon I'll pass beyond this changing vale*
> *To that which does not change.*
> *My tired feet will range*
> *In some green valley*
> *With eternal mind*
> *Where truth is daily,*
> *Like the water, soft.*

'Bloody good words, those!'

Harry's has been a wonderfully rich life, and in many ways he has changed plenty of lives himself through his endless encouragement and infectious laughter. Laughter that has brought both healing and happiness not only to himself, but also to millions around the world.

Thanks, Harry!

Laughter

Did you hear the little children laughing at their play,
*   today?*
Or catch the sound of merriment as others passed
*   your way?*
Was there something so amusing that the tears ran
*   down your face?*
Then thank the Lord for laughter, and the bounty of
*   his Grace,*
For laughter is a comma, that makes us pause in life,
That gives us welcome respite from our troubles, care
*   and strife.*
And when it's shared with others it's as golden as the
*   sun,*
Lighting up our darkest corners and uplifting
*   everyone.*
The clown, the wit, comedian, as each one plays his
*   part,*
Spends a lifetime giving, and that giving from the
*   heart,*

*And we would keep them centre stage and clap and
    cry, 'Encore',
And when they've given of their best we'd have them
    give some more.
These are the Laughter Makers, a precious, gifted
    breed,
And you, our dear Sir Harry, are a Prince of Mirth,
    indeed.*

ANNE BISSETT

Harry's Hymns and Halos

The years of Highway *and* Songs of Praise *added
many hymns and readings to Harry's list of favourites.
Here is a selection of his best-loved ones, sung or read by
him on the programme or by one of his guests. The
following prayer and poem are Harry's own, and are
followed by his own selection of favourite hymns beginning
with his all-time favourite.*

*O Lord,
Support us all the day long of this troubled life, until
the shades lengthen and the evening comes, the busy
world is hushed, the fever of life is over, and our work
done. Then Lord, in thy mercy grant me safe lodging,
a holy rest and peace at the last.
Through Jesus Christ our Lord.
Amen.*

Time traveller

*Sir Harry reflects on growing old in a piece that he wrote
specially for* Songs of Praise.

I want the mornings to last longer
And the twilight to linger.
I want to clutch the present to my bosom
And never let it go.
I resent the tyranny of the clock in the hall
Nagging me to get on with the day.
I am a time traveller
But a traveller who would rather walk
Than fly.
And yet:
There is a lot to be said for growing old.
The major battles in life are over
Though minor skirmishes may still occur
There is an armistice of the heart,
A truce with passion.
Compromise becomes preferable to conflict
And old animosities blur with time.
There is still one last hurdle to cross
And the joy of your life measures your
Reluctance to approach it.
But if you have lived your life with love
There will be nothing to fear
Because a warm welcome will await you
On the other side.

The Day Thou Gavest, Lord, is Ended

Harry has chosen this hymn as his all-time favourite, and,
it was his mother's favourite too. It was chosen by Queen
Victoria to be sung in every church on the occasion of her
Diamond Jubilee.

The day thou gavest, Lord, is ended
The darkness falls at thy behest
To thee our morning hymns ascended
Thy praise shall sanctify our rest

We thank thee that thy church unsleeping
While earth rolls onward into light
Through all the world her watch is keeping
And rests not now by day or night

As o'er each continent and island
The dawn leads on another day
The voice of prayer is never silent
Nor flies the strain of praise away

The sun that bids us rest is waking
Our brethren 'neath the western sky
And hour by hour fresh lips are making
Thy wondrous doings heard on high

So be it, Lord, thy throne shall never
Like earth's proud empires, pass away
Thy kingdom stands and grows forever
Till all thy creatures own thy sway.

J. ELLERTON (1826–93)

How Sweet the Name of Jesus Sounds

Slave trader John Newton's first set of compositions were
so full of bad language they are unprintable! After his
conversion, however, his mouth was washed with a
spiritual bar of soap and his hymns have become firm
favourites with many, including Sir Harry, who now hums
this to himself every morning.

SECOMBE ON SECOMBE

How sweet the name of Jesus sounds
In a believer's ear!
It soothes his sorrows, heals his wounds,
And drives away his fear.

It makes the wounded spirit whole
And calms the troubled breast;
'Tis manna to the hungry soul
And to the weary, rest.

Dear name, the rock on which I build
My shield and hiding place
My never failing treasury, filled
With boundless stores of grace

Jesus! My Shepherd, Saviour, Friend,
My Prophet, Priest and King,
My Lord, my Life, my Way, my End
Accept the praise I bring.

Weak is the effort of my heart
And cold my warmest thought
But when I see thee as thou art
I'll praise thee as I ought.

Till then I would thy love proclaim
With every fleeting breath:
And may the music of thy name
Refresh my soul in death.

JOHN NEWTON (1725–1807)

Death is Nothing At All

This poem, written by Canon Henry Scott Holland (1847–1918), became a favourite with viewers and Harry alike, and brought much comfort to those who had experienced bereavement. Harry read it many times.

Death is nothing at all – I have only slipped away into the next room – I am I and you are you – whatever we were to each other, that we are still. Call me by my old familiar name; speak to me in the easy way, which you always used. Put no difference into your tone; wear no forced air of solemnity or sorrow. Laugh as we always laughed at the little jokes we enjoyed together. Play, smile, think of me, pray for me.

Let my name be ever the household word that it always was. Let it be spoken without effect, without the ghost of a shadow on it. Life means all that it ever meant. It is the same as it ever was, there is absolutely unbroken continuity. What is this death but a negligible accident? Why should I be out of mind because I am out of sight? I am just waiting for you, for an interval, somewhere very near, just around the corner ... All is well.

Harry's Verse

Harry's faith has been an essential part of his ethos
throughout his long career. His spiritual gift is certainly
one of encouragement, something that everyone who has
met him has benefited from. Here is a verse which points
out the importance of this; it is the same one adopted by the
organization Christians in Entertainment.

Let us not give up the habit of meeting together, as some
are doing. Instead let us encourage one another all the
more, since you see that the day of the Lord is coming
nearer.

Hebrews 10:25 GNB

Sensational Secombe – Harry's Highlights

With a career that has taken in every possible
entertainment medium, Harry has an impressive
curriculum vitae! Here are just some of the highlights of
fifty years in show-biz, along with some of Harry's best-
loved shows, theatres, reviews and some significant dates.

The London Palladium

Harry's love of this famous theatre started when he first
imagined what it would be like to perform there. His dream
came true in 1951 when he was invited to appear in the
Royal Command Performance. Since then he has starred in
many royal shows, and appeared there on numerous other
occasions. The Palladium is still Harry's favourite theatre,
and Ronald Bergan in his book The Great Theatres Of
London explains why it is so well loved.

Life Begins At Oxford Circus And Round About Regent Street, the title of a 1935 Crazy Gang show at the London Palladium, just about summed up what lovers of the music hall or variety felt when approaching this enormous edifice of entertainment. For a variety act to have played the Palladium was equal in theatrical mythology to playing a two-a-day at Broadway's Palace Theatre. A list of all the famous stars that have appeared there would make up a 'Who's Who' of show business.

The vast, richly adorned and gilded auditorium with its two cantilevered balconies became familiar to millions on TV from the mid-1950s on with a weekly variety show broadcast called *Sunday Night At The London Palladium*. The MCs over the years included Tommy Trinder, Norman Vaughan, Bruce Forsyth and Jimmy Tarbuck. The formula was revived for a new generation in 1987 with *Live From The Palladium* hosted by Tarbuck.

Those who have had the pleasure of going to this theatre can testify to the surprising intimacy and atmosphere of the place. This People's Palace can claim, with a seating capacity of over 2,300, to be the largest live theatre in London, discounting only the Coliseum – slightly bigger but now an opera house. *The Era* of 1910 noted: 'Perhaps the most unique feature is the box-to-box telephone that has been installed. It will therefore be possible for the occupants of one box, recognizing friends in another box, to enter into conversation with them.' Alas, this little convenience no longer exists, and waving and shouting must suffice from the paired boxes on each level in arched niches.

The Palladium opened on 26 December 1910 with a variety bill topped by Nellie Wallace, 'The Essence of Eccentricity', Ella Shields, and 'Mr Martin Harvey and his full company' in a one-act play called *Conspiracy*. Subsequent programmes mixed farce, ballet, opera, melodrama, song and comedy in two shows each evening and two matinees a week. Variety it was called and variety it was!

In 1930, the Royal Variety Show, in aid of the Entertainment Artists' Benevolent Fund, was instigated at the Palladium, and the theatre was used more than any other for this annual event.

Royal Variety Performances

Roy Hudd, a past chairman of the Entertainment Artists' Benevolent Fund, says, 'To a performer a Royal Variety Performance is the great accolade and certainly the most nerve-wracking "gig" he or she will ever have to tackle. I have had the agony and ecstasy four times, and believe me, it gets no easier.'

Harry has had the honour of appearing in a Royal Variety Performance eleven times, topping the bill on five occasions. Apart from the regular comperes, such as Max Bygraves, he has therefore appeared in the Royal Variety Performance more often than any other artist.

1951

Harry's first Royal Variety Performance was in 1951, as Lord (then plain Bernard) Delfont, producer of the show, describes:

> *This year's show at the Victoria Palace was widely regarded as a big success; 'immensely good' was the Queen's own verdict on the performance.*
>
> *A notable hit was the youthful Harry Secombe in pre-Goon days with his comic and straight singing, whose performance drew a good response from Princess Margaret. Continuing the relatively new concept of a*

'warm-up' act was the Crazy Gang who, among other antics, dressed up as Beefeaters to greet the Royal Party on the stairs.

Other star turns were radio stars Richard Murdoch and Kenneth Horne of Much Binding in the Marsh, *the country's top woman impressionist, Florence Desmond, and singer Carole Lynne, my wife!*

1956

Harry was asked again five years later in 1956, on Guy Fawkes Night, but as Lord Delfont relates:

Perhaps it was just as well that 1955 had two Royal Variety Performances, for the 1956 one has gone down in history as the show that never was.

After the months of careful planning, the painstaking vetting of acts and the gruelling demands of bringing together all the disparate elements in less than forty-eight hours before its start, the unimaginable happened and the show was cancelled within four hours of curtain-up.

The cause lay far away in the Middle East, on the banks of the Suez Canal where British troops had landed that morning in Port Said, following previous operations in the past few days against military targets in Egypt. The Soviet Union was threatening to retaliate with rockets unless the British and French forces accepted a ceasefire and, as Val Parnell told a stunned cast as they were finishing their rehearsals, Her Majesty felt unable to attend in the mounting international crisis.

There was widespread disappointment among the cast. The Crazy Gang had specially put together a burlesque of A Midsummer Night's Dream. *Laurence*

Olivier, Vivien Leigh and John Mills were on the bill.
And Liberace had spent nine days travelling to
London for the show – first overland from Los Angeles
to New York and then by ship to Southampton. He felt
the disappointment keenly and wept openly.

Harry was already resident in the Number One dressing room, and in true Harry style opened up his drinks cabinet to help drown their sorrows at suffering such a huge anti-climax. It took some effort to console Liberace, but somehow Harry, along with Max Bygraves and Eric Sykes, eventually managed it.

1957

Harry was thrilled to be asked back the following year, by which time he had firmly established himself with the Goons. Strangely, in this show he was not featured as a comedian, but rather as a singer complete with the Morriston Orpheus Choir.

1958

Harry, invited back to appear for the third time in a decade, found himself sharing the stage with an array of talent including David Nixon, Charlie Drake, Eartha Kitt, Norman Wisdom, Rex Harrison, Stanley Holloway and Julie Andrews. Harry was also about to meet a new lifelong friend and a new star. It was to be a night that Harry would remember for the rest of his life. Mind you, as Lord Delfont remembers, so would Roy!

The Royal Variety Performance of 1958 marked the
first of the long-running series of Delfont/Nesbitt
productions and began the partnership that year at the
Coliseum with a large and impressive cast.

241

With shows like Where's Charlie? *at the Palace Theatre,* My Fair Lady *at Drury Lane and* The Merry Widow *at Sadler's Wells there was no shortage of first-rate material to draw on for the Royal Variety Show – and thanks to the revolving stage at the Coliseum it was possible to include a wide-ranging and impressive selection of numbers in the programme.*

1958 also marked the highly successful royal debut of Roy Castle, who was later to become such a big star of both stage and screen. 'He held the audience in the palm of his hand!!' said one glowing notice the following day.

Under the polished compering of Max Bygraves – a firm Royal Variety favourite by now – there was plenty of other talent to draw on, including Tony Hancock who appeared as a budgerigar in a cage above the stage! The much-loved Hattie Jacques playing the bird's owner joined him in the act.

The finale was truly spectacular, with Rex Harrison, Julie Andrews and Stanley Holloway singing songs from My Fair Lady *and ending with 'I Could Have Danced All Night', accompanied by no less than three orchestras on stage conducted by Mantovani, Victor Silvester and Cyril Stapleton, with yet another orchestra in the pit.*

1962

The first of Harry's involvements with the show in the sixties was to be special because his old wartime mate Norman Vaughan was to compere it for the first time. After opening by coming on stage in a real car, Harry stood in the wings and spurred Norman on as much as he dare without getting in the way of the enormous number of dancers, jugglers, comics and singers dashing around back-stage. They also had the chance to do a routine called 'Marching Orders' in which Norman Vaughan, Terry Kendall and Harry sent up the army. The Queen was most amused.

1963

The next year Harry was once again part of the annual event that the Lord Chamberlain initially refused to be allowed to be shown on television. His reasoning was that television might endanger variety theatres all over the country! The last but one Royal Variety Performance Harry had appeared in featured many of the latest musicals London had to offer; this time Harry was appearing in his own. *Pickwick* was running at the Saville Theatre, and Bernard Delfont wanted him to perform a couple of songs from the show. This he did alongside Tommy Steele's musical *Half A Sixpence*. Also on the bill were a new boy band, as Lord Delfont recalls:

> *This was the night when Beatlemania hit the Royal Variety Performance. By the early sixties the Fab Four from Liverpool were already big stars in the pop world and the presenters of the show at the Prince of Wales shrewdly realized it was time for their Royal show debut.*
>
> *Despite technical problems in rehearsals, it was decidedly more than 'all right on the night', with all the audience, including the Queen Mother, joining in with the beat. One commentator said, 'Never, in all my years of observing Royal Variety audiences, have I known this usually starchy, on-their-best behaviour bunch, unbend so quickly and so completely.'*
>
> *During rehearsal Paul McCartney managed to get his guitar caught in the curtains, but on the night*

itself the Beatles took the show by storm and John
Lennon passed into Royal Variety history when he
made his celebrated suggestion that those in the cheap
seats should clap their hands; the rest could just rattle
their jewellery.

The legendary Marlene Dietrich was also on the bill, along
with a varied parade of double acts including Michael
Flanders and Donald Swann, Steptoe and Son, and Pinky
and Perky.

1967

By the late sixties, Harry was becoming part of the furni-
ture as far as Royal Variety Performance audiences were
concerned. With his usual brand of relaxed good humour
and brilliant voice, Harry raised the roof at the Palladium
and not a few television sets around the country.

   Appearing with him were Rolf Harris, Lulu, Val
Doonican, Sandie Shaw, Ken Dodd, Tom Jones and Tommy
Cooper. Bob Hope brought the evening to a highly comical
climax.

1969

This year's 'RVP', as it is lovingly called, featured Des
O'Connor; Cilla Black, Danny La Rue, Moira Anderson,
Frankie Howerd and Ginger Rogers. Harry was to star
alongside his old mate Roy Castle and Ronnie Corbett was
to suffer an indignity. 'Ronnie Corbett was sporting a black
eye when he appeared before the Queen, and it was not a
joke!' Bernard Delfont says.

   The accident happened during a car crash as he was
   driven home after a night out. He recalled the incident
   with the precision of a rally driver: 'I was thrown

*against the fascia of the car. The rim of my glasses hit
me under the right eye.' However, Ronnie had the
good luck to be nursed by Danny La Rue, who bathed
the eye in champagne.*

*The advent of colour television posed new problems
for this show that were to be solved by somewhat
unusual methods. Thelma Taylor was the vital compo-
nent that helped ITV get the colour balance exactly
right. Ms Taylor, a dancer and singer by profession
(although not needing those skills for this particular
part), wore a green dress, pink stole and white boots.
If that didn't help the newfangled colour cameras,
nothing would!*

*A big hit of the evening was Danny La Rue. His act
was well received, especially his impersonations of
Margot Fonteyn and Sandie Shaw. Her Majesty the
Queen told him after the show, 'My gosh, your costume changes were fantastic. I only wish I could dress
as quickly as you.'*

1975

'It was *Billy*'s year as the incredibly versatile Michael
Crawford, with other members of the Drury Lane show, won
over the audience of the 1975 Royal Variety Performance at
the Palladium,' reported Lord Delfont.

*Crawford's talent and sheer ebullience certainly
pleased the Queen and Prince Philip in an evening of
wide-ranging talent.*

*For sheer scale the splendour of the Kwa Zulu
African song and dance company and the Rhos Male
Voice Choir from Wales, who featured in the finale
with Royal Variety veterans Harry Secombe and Vera
Lynn, made magnificent entertainment. More music*

245

came from Count Basie and his orchestra and light comedy from the team of the television series, Dad's Army. *One of the big hits of the night was the French singer, Charles Aznavour.*

There was something of a furore over whether the female dancers in Kwa Zulu could appear topless as they did in their West End show. What would the Queen think? Would she be offended? These questions were answered by a spokesperson from Buckingham Palace, very tactfully putting forward Her Majesty's reassurance that 'The Queen has seen topless ladies before.'

Michael Crawford made a death-defying entrance, travelling across the stage by means of a rope tied around one ankle. No wonder he was insured for £150,000 against accident!

1978
The Queen Mother presided over this year's royal event, which featured 'Harry's World of Music'. The King's Singers, Mary O'Hara and even pop group Showaddywaddy shared the stage with Harry that night.

1987
Cannon and Ball topped their first Royal Variety, which marked Harry's return to the show. Indeed it was an evening almost completely dedicated to comedy and starred Gary Wilmot, Peter Goodwright, Leslie Crowther, Bobby Davro, Les Dawson and the Roly Polys, Mike Yarwood, Jimmy Tarbuck, and Michael Barrymore. It made the house rock with laughter and epitomized all that Harry himself holds dear.

Television series

Apart from the one-off shows and guest appearances which are far too numerous to record here, what follows is a list of Harry's principal series since he first arrived on our screens in the mid-fifties.

1955
Secombe Here!

Harry had Jimmy Grafton, Eric Sykes and Spike Milligan as writers for his initial series of three one-hour shows. The first was broadcast in black and white at 9.30 p.m. and featured Johnny Vyvyan as guest and stooge. Also appearing were old mates Milligan and Sykes, with Sellers in the second show. The final show was broadcast live from the National Radio Show at Earl's Court and was followed by a variety special in which Harry took part.

The Harry Secombe Show

With a show initially transmitted just two days after the launch of ITV, Harry was the first star to attract his own weekly series on the new commercial network. Two specials featuring Norman Vaughan and Johnny Vyvyan followed a series of six forty-five-minute shows, all written by Eric Sykes.

1957
The Secombe Saga

The BBC managed to snatch Harry back for this one-off special written by Eric Sykes, with new variety man Ernest Maxim, later to become famous for his Morecambe and Wise shows, producing.

1958
This Is Your Life
The first time Harry was caught, with his parents as special guests. Hosted by Eamonn Andrews.

1959
Secombe and Friends
The first of Harry's main Saturday night slots, transmitted at 7.55 p.m., which were aired over a period of eight years. This was a series of single shows concentrating on Goon-like comedy and featured Harry's fellow Goons, along with other guests including Lionel Blair, Harry Worth, Richard Burton, Roy Castle, Tony Hancock and Danny La Rue.

Secombe At Large
Two editions of this one-hour stand-up show went out in May and November respectively and featured a mixed bag of music and comedy with Sam Kydd, Dora Bryan and Clive Dunn.

1963
Who Is Secombe?
Almost an alternative Boxing Day version of *This Is Your Life*, in which Harry is 'taught' to dance by Amanda Barrie, to be funny by Dora Bryan, to be sexy by Fenella Fielding, to be intellectual by Jimmy Edwards and be a good actor by Anton Rodgers.

1968–72
The Harry Secombe Show
A major new series marking the climax of Harry's television career. Four series of thirty-one shows went out on prime-time TV over four years. These were varied in

nature; some were musically focused, while others were comedy led.

1969
Pickwick
On 11 June Harry's highly successful stage musical was brought to the small screen in this TV version.

1973
Sing a Song of Secombe
A series of musical trips included this one-off recording.

Bombardier Secombe – Back Among The Boys
A filmed recording of Harry entertaining troops in Northern Ireland.

1977
Have a Harry ...
Have a Harry Christmas and *Have a Harry Birthday* were two of the ingenious titles in this series of specials in which ITV won Harry back for their major TV line-up after an absence of twenty-two years.

Secombe's slow drift of emphasis away from comedy and towards music was to prepare him for a whole range of musical specials, as well as the longest-running single series of his career.

1983–92
Highway
Originally feeling ill-suited to this idea – 'How can a raspberry-blowing Goon be taken seriously!' – Harry was to enjoy a ten-year stint on a programme that was not only obviously written for him, but which he was born to

present. It had a great personal effect on him, as it did the millions who watched each Sunday evening.

1990
This Is Your Life
Harry was doing a book signing when Michael Aspel jumped out from behind the piles of volumes and presented him with the big red book for the second time. 'You swine!' screamed Harry 'You've already done me once!'

ITV, who were now running the series, had become much more aware of the danger of 'leakages' to its subjects and had invented a new system of codenames. While Donald Sinden was 'Butler', Magnus Pike was 'Fish' and Esther Rantzen was 'Queen', somehow Harry's was codenamed 'Road'. Understandable, I suppose, in that he had travelled at least 25,000 miles up and down motorways that year presenting *Highway*.

1993–4
Sunday with Secombe
A two-hour live extension to *Highway*, this Sunday morning special travelled to a different setting each week. With various guests being interviewed or contributing songs or news items, this popular programme was co-hosted with Kaye Adams.

1995–9
Songs of Praise
As soon as Harry was free from his ITV contract, the BBC very rapidly snatched him up again. This time it was to present a series of one-off specials for their flagship Sunday show. Although he was seventy-four years old, the producers at the BBC were well aware that Harry was nowhere near his sell-by date (will he ever be?), and that his immense skill as a natural presenter was still a rarity.

2000
The Trouble with Harry
Harry wanted to use his experiences of illness as a way of bringing hope to other sufferers. In order to inform and encourage those dealing with the effects of cancer and stroke, Harry invited the same cameras that had seen him centre-stage now to view him in his incapacity. With Harry, however, there is always an up side, and the programme gives a hugely optimistic thrust towards not only coping with but also overcoming the huge hurdles that life can throw up before all of us.

There is no doubt that Harry will continue to use his gifts of television communication to exhort, encourage, hearten, inspire and to press us forward on our own life journey on a carpet of laughter and fun.

Chronology

It would not be possible to mention all the many thousands of appearances that Harry has made, but here are just some of the highlights of his life and fifty-year-plus career in show business:

1921
Harry Secombe born 8 September

1946
Windmill Theatre
Germany variety tour
Variety Bandbox, BBC Radio
Grand Theatre, Bolton

1947
Dick Whittington, East Ham Palace
Forces Showboat

1948
Marriage to Myra, 19 February, at St Barnabas Church, Sketty, Swansea
Forces Showboat tour

1949
Rooftop Rendezvous, BBC Television live broadcast, New Year's Day
Third Division, BBC Radio
The Cyril Fletcher Show, BBC Television
Summer season with Cyril Fletcher, Pavilion Theatre, Torquay
Welsh Rarebit, BBC Radio
Toad of Toad Hall, BBC Television

1950
Dick Whittington, New Theatre, Hull

1951
Opera House, Blackpool
First 'Goon show' recorded Sunday 27 May and transmitted the following day as *The Junior Crazy Gang*, BBC Radio
The Junior Crazy Gang renamed *Crazy People* and becomes a weekly series, BBC Radio
First Royal Variety Performance, Victoria Palace, London

1952
Listen My Children, BBC Radio
Third Division, BBC Radio

1953
Educating Archie, BBC Radio, with ventriloquist Peter Brough and his dummy Archie Andrews
Hancock's Half Hour: Harry took over from Tony, who was indisposed. With Sid James and Kenneth Williams

1954
Svengali, first major feature film

1955
Secombe Here, first major series on BBC Television

1956
The Ed Sullivan Show, US television
Rocking the Town, debut appearance at the London Palladium, May
Royal Variety Performance, London Palladium, with Liberace – cancelled due to the Suez crisis

1958
Royal Variety Performance, London Palladium, with the then unknown Roy Castle
First *This Is Your Life*, with Eamonn Andrews
Large as Life, Palladium variety revue with Terry-Thomas, Eric Sykes, Hattie Jacques and Harry Worth

1959
Humpty Dumpty, London Palladium pantomime
Jet Storm, Pinewood Studios with Dame Sybil Thorndyke
Secombe and Friends, one-hour weekly special for BBC Television which ran for three years

1960
Final *Goon Show*, January

1961
Let Yourself Go, London Palladium variety revue, with Roy Castle and Ronnie Corbett

1962
Royal Variety Performance, London Palladium

1963
CBE awarded
Royal Variety Performance, Prince of Wales Theatre with Marlene Dietrich and The Beatles
Pickwick opens at Palace Theatre, Manchester, transferring to Saville Theatre, London

1965
Pickwick opens in San Francisco, tours the USA and finishes on Broadway with Tony nomination

1966
London Laughs, London Palladium with Jimmy Tarbuck, Thora Hird and Anita Harris

1967
Royal Variety Performance, London Palladium
The Four Musketeers, Drury Lane, London

1968
Oliver!, feature film starring Ron Moody, Mark Lester, Jack Wild, Peggy Mount, Shani Wallis and Oliver Reed

1972
The Last Goon Show of All, special celebratory recording, 5 October

1975
The Plumber's Progress, musical play, Prince of Wales Theatre, London

1981
Awarded knighthood in May

1983
Highway first conceived and broadcast

1990
This Is Your Life, the second time, with Michael Aspel

1992
Pickwick, national tour with Roy Castle

1993
Sunday with Secombe, successor to *Highway* which became a popular live Sunday magazine programme

1995
Songs of Praise – Harry joins the BBC's team and hosts many of its specials, including several Remembrance Days

1999
The Trouble with Harry, Medwyn Hughes documentary on Harry's illness

Recordings
'On with the Motley' – first 78 rpm single (Philips, 1955), reached no. 16 in the charts
'If I Ruled the World' (Philips, 1963), reached no. 16 in the charts
'This is My Song' (Philips, 1967), reached no. 2 in the charts

This is My Song compilation album (Spectrum Music, 1994)
Oliver! cast recording (Columbia, 1993)
Pickwick cast recording (Showtime, 1995)
Numerous other compilations

Books

Twice Brightly (Robson Books, 1974, reissued 1999), a show-biz novel
Welsh Fargo (Robson Books, 1981), hilarity caused by a small bus company in South Wales
Katy and the Nurgla (Robson Books, 1980), a children's story about a monster that lives in the sea
The Nurgla's Magic Tear (Robson Books, 1991), another children's novel, sequel to the above
Goon for Lunch (Michael Joseph, 1975), Harry's reflections on the series that became a comedy classic
Goon Abroad (Robson Books, 1982), more memories of the Goons
Arias and Raspberries (Robson Books, 1989), the first volume of Harry's autobiography
Strawberries and Cheam (Robson Books, 1996), the autobiography, volume two
Harry Secombe Diet Book (Robson Books, 1983), encouraging weight loss Harry's way
Harry Secombe's Highway (Robson Books, 1985), a look behind the scenes of one of television's most popular series
The Highway Companion (Robson Books, 1987), a collection of stories, anecdotes and excerpts from the series
Harry Secombe's Zoo Loo Book (Robson Books, 1999), Harry's limericks with illustrations by Bill Tidy

Harry on the Web

Thousands enjoyed the experience of seeing *Pickwick*. They include many who still post their memories of several years ago on the internet, like this one from *mickie@tellecall.co.uk*;

Acclaimed entertainer Sir Harry Secombe returned to the stage at the Bristol Hippodrome to resurrect his role as Samuel Pickwick in a musical based on Charles Dickens' novel The Pickwick Papers.

It is a role he originated more than thirty years ago, and the song 'If I Ruled the World' became a hit single for Harry in the 1960s. Now in his seventies, the former Goon still behaves like a walking bomb, with bursts of infectious laughter or the sudden outbreak of a goonish voice peppering his conversation.

Commenting on the play's revival, Harry said: 'To return after thirty years is a bit of a liberty, really. I wasn't sure I could do it again. I was rung up and asked to do it so I had a chat with my family – some of them weren't even born when I did it before – and I thought about it and said I'd have a bash.

'We did a season at Chichester and it grew from there into a tour. It keeps a lot of people working, too.'

Tenor Harry, who presented the top-rated Highway *on TV for ten years, said: 'This is the kind of show you can take the kids to. It's not a pantomime and it's the other side of the coin from* Oliver!. *Dickens was a great writer. He wrote great characters – not unlike the characters in* The Goon Show: *Snodgrass, Winkle and Tupman.*

'It was originally written as text to accompany illustrations, published in weekly parts, but the text

took over and Seymour, the artist, eventually commit-
ted suicide. Because of that episodic broad canvas you
have to whittle it down to just one part and we
decided to hinge it on the breach of promise with Mrs
Bardell. So all the best characters are in.'

Harry's enthusiasm for the show and its company
is enormous: 'It's a good romp. The energy of the com-
pany is tremendous and at my time of life it's like
lying on a feather bed with all these people pushing me
up.'

Other Secombe websites include:
http://www.goonshow.org.uk
http://www.britishcomedy.org.uk

Anagrams

With thanks to the internet's AnagramGenius.com, rearranging the letters of 'Sir Harry Secombe CBE' gives over 200 different titles. Many of them could be straight out of *The Goon Show*! These are the best:

My! He is a BBC sorcerer.
Access merrier hobby.
Messy, choicer barber.
By microbes research.
Robbery crashes mice.
He's crabby or mercies.
Come! bribery crashes.
Obey charmer scribes.
Mere heroics by crabs.
Merry, chic, sober base.
Besmirch yob careers.
Some crabby cherries.
Robbery chases crime.
Bribery screams echo.
By choicer, mere brass.
Bash by mice sorcerer.
Icy researcher bombs.
Chose scream bribery.

Crabby crimes, heroes.
Rim or crabby cheeses.
My bib aches sorcerer.
Yobs besmirch career.
Cheers! crabby or semi.
I'm cross-brace hereby.
Cheesy carrier bombs.
Cry bimbo researches.
Cheers! I'm cosy barber.
Merry crises ache bob.
By obese crier charms.
Besmirch cosy bearer.
Merry ice crashes bob.
So besmirch by career.
Oh! crabby, mere crises.

and many, many more ...

Index